RENAL DIET
COOKBOOK

The Ultimate Low Sodium, Low Potassium,

and Low Phosphorus Diet.

With a Complete Meal Plan and 200+ Delicious Renal-Friendly Recipes

SELMA OLSON

TABLE OF CONTENTS

INTRODUCTION

Keeping our kidneys healthy is a vital part of our general well-being.

The renal diet might be called the most cutting-edge healthy diet because it doesn't allow eating processed food. The main principle of the renal diet is to replace canned and processed foods with fresh or frozen fruits and vegetables.

Note that this diet limits the use of certain products, but the list of them is rather short. So, you will be able to enjoy your life without any solid limitations, regarding food and drinks.

Weak renal function is a quite spread condition in today's world; the main goal of this book is to help people improve their wellbeing by simply improving and being aware of the food they introduce to their bodies; by understanding what they really need from food, and reducing the intake of ingredients and food groups that may come as harmful for your kidney and renal health.

With a compilation of simple and easy recipes for breakfast, lunch, dinner, and snacks, this guide is designed to be an introduction to a healthy lifestyle, and an aid for you to enter a new chapter of your life.

Chapter 1

UNDERSTANDING KIDNEY DISEASE

How the Kidneys Work

Our kidneys are bean-shaped filters that work as a team. They have a very important job since they keep our bodies stable. They use specific signals from the body, like blood pressure and sodium content, to help keep us hydrated and our blood pressure stable.

Dysfunctional kidneys may result in numerous problems: when the filtration of toxins gets slower, harmful chemicals—present too often in our grocery list—can build up and cause defensive reactions within the body like vomiting, nausea, and rashes. When the kidney's functions continue to decrease, its ability to get rid of water and release blood pressure to control hormones can also be affected. As a consequence, symptoms such as high blood pressure or swollen feet caused by water retention might ensue. A prolonged and persistent reduced kidney function could cause long-term health problems such as osteoporosis or anemia.

Our kidneys work hard, so we have to protect them because they can filter around 120 to 150 quarts of blood each day. This will create between 1 and 2 quarts of urine that are made up of excess fluid and waste products.

What It Means To Have CKD

It is going to sound scary when you get diagnosed with chronic kidney disease and you probably have a lot of questions. This disease can be managed very well. It will take some exploration, patience, and time to see the big picture. Your first step to managing kidney disease is being able to understand it. Let's take a look at the role your kidneys play in your health, how your diet plays an important role in helping to manage kidney disease, and what happens when you develop kidney disease.

Once you have been diagnosed with CKD, it will be helpful to explore this disease and learn about some normal symptoms. A simple definition is a gradual loss of the function of your kidneys. Because our bodies constantly produce waste, our kidneys play a big role to remove these toxins and keep our system working properly. Tests will be done to measure the level of waste in your blood and figure out how well your kidneys are working. Your doctor will be able to find out the filtration rate of your kidneys and figure out what stage of CKD you are in.

Five stages show how the kidneys function. Within the early stages, people won't experience any symptoms, and it is very easy to manage. Oftentimes, kidney disease isn't found until it becomes advanced. Most symptoms don't appear until the toxins buildup in the body from the damage that has been done to the kidneys, what usually happens in the later stages. Changes in how you urinate, vomiting, nausea, swelling, and itching could be caused by decreased ability to filtrate the toxins. This is why an early diagnosis that is critical to positive outcomes can come later when the disease has progressed.

There isn't a cure for CKD, but you can manage this disease. Making changes to your lifestyle and diet can slow down the progression and help you stay away from symptoms that normally start to show up later. These lifestyle changes can improve your total health and allow you to manage other conditions. Once you begin making changes to your daily food habits, you will see improvement in these conditions including diabetes and hypertension.

You can live a happy, healthy, and long life while managing CKD, and making changes early can slow down the progression of this disease for years.

Chronic Kidney Disease (CKD)

This is the most common form of kidney disease in humans. Chronic Kidney Disease (CKD) is a long-term, progressive condition that can affect anyone – young or old. The most common cause of CKD is hypertension or high blood pressure. Hypertension can increase the pressure on the glomeruli, the tiny blood vessels in the kidneys that filtrate the blood. It is extremely harmful to the kidneys and can lead to impaired kidney function over time. When the kidneys are no longer functioning dialysis is needed to filter wastes and extra fluids out of the blood. If the condition worsens, a kidney transplant may be needed.

Another major cause of CKD is diabetes, a group of diseases that results in abnormal (usually high) blood sugar levels. This is extremely harmful because it damages the blood vessels of the kidneys. Damaged blood vessels can impair the main function of the kidneys – filtering out wastes in the blood. When your body becomes loaded with so many wastes, kidney failure is more likely to occur.

Kidney Stones

Kidney stones, also called renal calculi, are solid masses of crystals that originate in the kidneys. This is a common kidney condition that occurs when nutrients and other substances in the blood crystallize and form stones in the kidneys. Kidney stones cause renal colic or severe, excruciating pain on either one side of the back or abdomen. These stone crystals are normally excreted out of the body during urination.

Glomerulonephritis

It is also called inflammation of the glomeruli, the tiny structures inside the kidney that filter the blood. This disease is commonly caused by drugs, kidney infection, and birth anomalies or birth defects. Glomerulonephritis is a type of kidney disease that often resolves on its own.

Polycystic Kidney Disease (PKD)

Polycystic kidney disease is an inherited kidney problem that is manifested by the formation of cysts or small sacs of fluid in the kidneys. These cysts interfere with the normal functioning of the kidneys that can lead to kidney failure.

Urinary Tract Infections (UTI)

These are bacterial infections of the upper and lower urinary tract. The most common forms of UTI are infections in the urethra and bladder. UTI can be easily treated using antibacterial medications and increased fluid intake. But if left untreated, these infections can result in more serious complications such as kidney failure.

Kidney Failure

Kidney failure is a severe condition that happens when your kidneys lose their ability to filter waste products from your blood. This is also referred to as End-Stage Renal Disease (ESRD) or End-Stage Kidney Disease. When your kidneys stop functioning, it is more likely that you will undergo dialysis treatment or a kidney transplant. Common causes of kidney disease include diabetes, hypertension, autoimmune diseases, nephrotic syndrome, and urinary tract problems.

The 5 Stages of Kidney Failure

Stage 1

Stage 1 is referred to as a very mild stage. Patients may become asymptomatic and there is a smaller risk for possible complications. Stage 1 can be managed by following a healthy lifestyle. For patients who have diabetes, they need to check their blood sugar levels regularly.

Stage 2

Stage 2 is still classified as a mild form of kidney disease. A person may experience having proteinuria or the presence of protein in the urine. Other physical damages to the kidneys may also be more obvious. A healthy lifestyle and a regular checkup with your doctor are the two most important management practices at this stage.

Stage 3

Stage 3 is already considered a moderate stage of kidney disease. At this stage, the kidneys aren't working as efficiently as before. Symptoms are more visible such as swelling in the upper and lower extremities, and frequent urination. A good lifestyle with some prescribed medications is required during this stage.

Stage 4

Stage 4 is classified as a moderate to severe stage of kidney disease. The kidneys are mostly not functioning properly, but it is not yet considered complete kidney failure. Most of the evident symptoms may include high blood pressure, anemia, and bone disorders. Together with a healthy lifestyle, medications and treatments are the most common forms of management at this stage.

Stage 5

Stage 5 is considered as the stage of nearly complete or total kidney failure. Different manifestations of the loss of kidney function such as nausea and vomiting, difficulty breathing, rash, and seizures are more evident. Regular dialysis treatment and kidney transplants are extremely needed at this stage. If not properly managed, this can lead to sudden death.

Treatment Options for Kidney Failure

The following are the most common treatments for people with kidney failure:

Dialysis

This is a treatment that is performed to filter and purify the blood using a specialized machine. A dialysis machine performs the same function as the human kidneys. Depending on the severity of your condition, you may be required to undergo dialysis treatment once a week or 2-3 times weekly. People should understand that dialysis treatment doesn't cure the disease, it only helps you extend your life.

Kidney Transplant

A kidney transplant is another option that can be used to treat kidney failure. A person who received a new kidney can go back to their normal routine and dialysis is no longer needed. It is normally a long process before a person with kidney failure can get a compatible donor. After the transplant, you are required to take immunosuppressive drugs to prevent your body from rejecting the newly introduced kidney. A kidney transplant may not be for everyone, especially for those who have compromised immunity. It is best to talk to your doctor about this procedure.

Kidney-friendly diet or renal diet

Please refer to the previous chapter.

Prevention and Home Remedies

Kidney diseases, especially kidney failure, may be prevented by:

- Following and maintaining a healthy lifestyle

- Limiting or avoiding foods that are high in sodium, potassium, and phosphorous

- Not suppressing urination

- Treating early symptoms of kidney disease

- Taking prescribed medications for chronic diseases

- Following your physician's advice

What To Eat and What To Avoid in Renal Diet

Food to Avoid

Food with high sodium content:

- Onion salt, marinades, garlic salt, teriyaki sauce, and table salt

- Pepperoni, bacon, ham, lunch meat, hot dogs, sausage, processed meats

- Ramen noodles, canned produce, and canned soups

- Marinara sauce, gravy, salad dressings, soy sauce, BBQ sauce, and ketchup

- Chex Mix, salted nuts, Cheetos, crackers, and potato chips

- Fast food

Food with a high potassium level:

- Fruits: dried fruit, oranges/orange juice, prunes/prune juice, kiwi, nectarines, dates, cantaloupe, bananas, black currants, damsons, cherries, grapes, and apricots.

- Vegetables: tomatoes/tomato sauce/tomato juice, sweet potatoes, beans, lentils, split peas, spinach (cooked), pumpkin, potatoes, mushrooms (cooked), chile peppers, chard, Brussels sprouts (cooked), broccoli (cooked), baked beans, avocado, butternut squash, and acorn squash.

- Protein and other foods: peanut butter, molasses, granola, chocolate, bran, sardines, fish, bacon, ham, nuts and seeds, yogurt, milkshakes, and milk.

- Coconut-based snacks, nut-based snacks, fudge, and toffee.

- Cakes containing marzipan.

- Potato crisps.

Foods with high phosphorus:

- Dairy products: pudding, ice cream, yogurt, cottage cheese, cheese, and milk.

- Nuts and seeds: sunflower seeds, pumpkin seeds, pecans, peanut butter, pistachios, cashews, and almonds.

- Dried beans and peas: soybeans, split peas, refried beans, pinto beans, lentils, kidney beans, garbanzo beans, black beans, and baked beans.

- Meat: veal, turkey, liver, lamb, beef, bacon, fish, and seafood.

- Carbohydrates: whole grain products, oatmeal, and bran cereals.

What to eat

- Drinks: You can favor the following drinks in your renal diet: some water, citrus-based juices, wine, cranberry juice. Please consult with your doctor to know the right number of fluids you should drink, depending on your kidney conditions and the treatments you are going under. Don't forget to include the liquids included in soups or other liquid dishes.

- Eat Plenty of Vegetables: Corn, carrot, cabbage peas, eggplants, celery, lettuce, asparagus, bean sprouts, red bell peppers, onions, garlic, and cauliflower.

- Choose Low Sugar Fruits: Cranberries, apples, cherries, blackberries, blueberries, mangoes, pears, peaches, and grapes.

- Others: Privilege olive oil to other oils, eggs, lean meats such as poultry, beef, pork, coriander, ginger.

Tips To Slow Kidney Disease and How To Avoid Dialysis

Having a positive attitude is important and the way you embrace the steps will determine how you manage your kidney disease. With some determination and willpower from you, you will soon be in charge of your destiny and health.

Commit

You might begin feeling a bit overwhelmed when you think about this disease. Take a few deep breaths. Everything is going to be fine because you've got this. Just like any life change, creating new habits will take time. Start preparing yourself mentally by telling yourself that you can control this disease by managing your lifestyle and diet.

Be determined to change your lifestyle and habits. Your commitment to yourself and your motivation to follow through will help you manage your kidney disease. Keep in mind that the earlier this disease gets detected, the better you can treat it. There is a goal for your treatment: slowing down the disease and keeping it from getting any worse. This is one good thing about kidney disease: it lets you take control so you can manage it.

Some good health practices

- Make sure to exercise daily
- Try to avoid smoking altogether
- Keep your diabetes in check
- Keep your blood pressure in check
- Try to stay on a job that you love doing and keep your health insurance
- Always consult with the individuals who are taking care of your health, such as your doctor, and follow their advice
- Try not to overeat and keep your weight in check
- Always try to avoid adding more salt to your diet
- Try to avoid excess sugar
- Try to be socially active as it will help to lighten your mood
- And above all, do the things that you love and try to stay positive all the time.

Know Your Nutritional Needs

There isn't one diet plan that will be right for everybody who has kidney disease. What you can eat is going to change with time. It all depends on how well your kidneys function and factors such as being a diabetic. If you work closely with a health team and constantly learn how to be able to make healthy choices that fit your needs, you can manage your disease and be successful.

Basic Guidelines That Are Useful for Anyone Who Has Chronic Kidney Disease:

Protein

Protein is present in animal and plant foods. It is a macronutrient that is needed for a healthy body. Too much protein isn't good for the body. As the function of the kidneys declines, the body can't get rid of the waste that gets produced when protein gets broken down and begins to build up in the blood. The correct amount of protein depends on what stage your kidney disease is in, your body size, appetite, levels of albumin, and other factors. A dietitian could help you figure out your daily limits of protein intake. You need to eat 37 to 41 grams of protein daily.

Fats

When you are going through times where you have to restrict what you eat, it is good to know that being able to eat healthy fats is another macronutrient that you need to include daily. Eating healthy fats makes sure you are getting all the essential fatty acids that can help your body in many ways. Polyunsaturated and monounsaturated fats are both unsaturated fats but they are healthy fats because of their benefits to the heart like decreasing LDL, increasing HDL, and lowering the total cholesterol levels. The correct types of fat might decrease inflammation within the body and will protect your kidney from more damage. You should try to include small amounts of these fats into your daily diet.

Carbohydrates

Carbs are another macronutrient that the body needs. This is what the body uses for energy. They also give the body many minerals, fiber, and vitamins that help protect the body. The body needs 130 grams of carbs daily for normal function.

Sodium

Consuming too much sodium makes you thirsty. This can cause increased blood pressure and swelling. Having high blood pressure could cause even more damage to the kidneys that are already unhealthy. Consuming less sodium will lower blood pressure and could slow down chronic kidney disease. The normal recommendation for anyone who has CKD is to keep their sodium intake around 2,000 mg daily. To have the best success is remembering that eating fresh is the best.

Potassium

Potassium can be found in many beverages and foods. It has an important role. It regulates the heartbeat and keeps muscles functioning. People who have kidneys that aren't healthy will need to limit their intake of foods that will increase potassium in the blood to dangerous levels. Eating a diet that restricts your level of potassium means eating around 2,000 milligrams each day. Consult your doctor to know the appropriate potassium levels based on your individual needs and blood work.

To lessen the buildup of potassium, you have to know what foods are low and high in potassium. This way you know what foods to be careful around.

Phosphorus

Healthy kidneys can help the body regulate phosphorus. When you have CKD, your kidneys can't remove excess phosphorus or get rid of it. This results in high levels of phosphorus in the blood and causes the body to pull calcium from bones. This, in turn, will lead the brittle and weak bones. Having elevated levels of calcium and phosphorus could lead to dangerous mineral deposits in the soft tissues of the body. This is called calciphylaxis.

Phosphorus can be found naturally in plant and animal proteins and larger levels are present in processed foods. By choosing foods that are low in phosphorus will keep the phosphorus levels in your body safe. The main rule to keep from eating unwanted phosphorus goes back to the "fresh is the best" concept. Stay away from all processed foods. Normal phosphorus intake for anyone who has CKD needs to be around 800 to 1,000 milligrams daily.

Supplements and Vitamins

Instead of relying on supplements, you need to follow a balanced diet. This is the best way to get the number of vitamins your body needs each day. Because of the restrictive CKD diet, it can be hard to get the necessary nutrients and vitamins you need. Anyone who has CKD will have greater needs for vitamins that are water-soluble. Certain renal supplements are needed to get the needed extra water-soluble vitamins. Renal vitamins could be small doses of vitamin C, biotin, pantothenic acid, niacin, folic acid, Vitamins B12, B6, B2, and B1.

The kidney converts inactive vitamin D to active vitamin D so our bodies can use it. With CKD, kidneys lose the ability to do this. Your health care provider could check your parathyroid hormone, phosphorus, and calcium levels to figure out if you need to take any supplements of active vitamin D. This type of vitamin D requires a prescription.

If your doctor hasn't prescribed a supplement, don't hesitate to ask them if you would benefit from one. To help keep you healthy, only use supplements that have been approved by your dietitian or doctor.

Fluids

The main function of the kidney is to regulate the balance of fluids in the body. For many individuals who have CKD, you don't have to restrict your fluid intake if your output is normal. An increase in the disease contributes to a decline in output and an increase in retention. If this happens, restricting fluids will become necessary. You have to pay attention to how much fluid you are releasing. Let your health care team know if your output is declining. They will be able to tell you how much fluid you should limit daily to keep healthy fluid levels to prevent an overload of fluid in the body along with other complications that are associated with extra fluid buildups like congestive heart failure, pulmonary edema, and high blood pressure.

Understand Your Calorie Requirements

Each person's calorie requirements will be different, and it doesn't matter if they do or don't have CKD. If they do have CKD, picking the correct foods, and eating the right number of calories will help your body. Calories give us the energy to function daily. They can help to slow the progression of kidney disease, keep a healthy weight, avoid losing muscle mass, prevent infections. Eating too many calories could cause weight gain, and that can put more of a burden on your kidneys. You must get the correct number of calories. The amount of calories for a person with CKD is about 60 to 70 calories per pound of body weight. If you weigh about 150 pounds, you need to consume around 2,000 calories per day.

Read Food Labels

It takes time to learn the renal diet and make it a part of your life. Lucky for you, all packaged foods come with nutrition labels along with an ingredient list. You need to read these labels so you can choose the right foods for your nutrition needs.

The major ingredients to check on labels are potassium, phosphorus, sodium, and fat. Food manufacturers should list the sodium and fat content of the food as required by law. They aren't required to list potassium or phosphorus. It is important to find this information in other places like the internet or books.

Portion Control

When you have kidney disease, controlling your portions is important. This doesn't mean you have to starve yourself. It doesn't matter what stage of CKD you are in but eating moderately is important when preserving your kidney health. The biggest part is making sure you don't feel deprived. You can enjoy many different foods as long as they are kidney-friendly and don't overeat. When you cut back on foods that could harm your health and you are careful about what you eat, you are learning portion control. Make a habit of limiting specific foods and eating in moderation when following a kidney diet. It just requires having an informed game plan, determination, and time.

HOW TO TEST FOR KIDNEY DISEASE

Glomerular filtration rate (GFR)

A test that determines whether your kidneys are both working efficiently and if not, determining which stage of kidney disease you may have.

A blood creatinine test

It is performed to test your levels of creatinine in the blood. Creatinine is a waste product that gets released into the blood when broken down, which could be dangerous for your health and have a very negative effect on your kidneys.

Ultrasound/CT scan

These image-based tests can take clear images of your organs, particularly your kidneys, to see whether they look and function properly. This test can help doctors identify whether your kidneys are the right size and whether they have structural problems.

Kidney biopsy

This test is performed during sedation and is done by removing a tissue sample from the kidneys, which can indicate the health and damage of the organs.

URINE TEST

As the simplest test to check whether your kidneys and other bodily processes are healthy, the urine test can help a doctor see whether your kidneys are infected or damaged.

CAUSES OF CKD

Different reasons can cause acute kidney failure. These would include any condition that would slow down the supply of blood to your kidneys, any direct damage to the kidney, or when the urine drainage tubes in the kidneys have been blocked because of the accumulation of waste in the body.

The first cause could be an impairment of the flow of blood to the kidneys and this could be caused due to different diseases and conditions like loss of blood or fluid from your body, use of medication for regulating blood pressure, heart attack, and heart diseases, any infection, failure of the liver, excessive usage of drugs like aspirin, ibuprofen, naproxen and other similar drugs, a severe reaction to allergies, burns and excessive dehydration.

The second cause could be certain diseases, conditions, and agents that can cause severe damage to the kidneys and this would lead to acute failure of kidneys. Some of these diseases and conditions are mentioned here. If there are any blood clots in the blood vessels in and near the kidneys, blocking of the blood flow to the kidneys due to deposits of cholesterol, inflammation of the small filters present in kidneys, infection of any manner, destruction of red blood cells, lupus, particular medications like chemotherapy drugs, dyes that are used for testing and so on, cancer that targets the plasma cells, scleroderma, blood disorders, inflammation of blood vessels in the body and the presence of toxins like alcohol, cocaine and even heavy metals can cause severe damage to the kidneys.

The third cause would be the blockage of the passage of urine out of the body that can cause kidney failure. The conditions that can obstruct the passage of urine are bladder, cervical, prostate, or even colon cancer, blood clots in the urinary tract, enlargement of the prostate, kidney stones, and any damage to the nerves that regulate the bladder.

Kidney failure usually occurs along with or due to another medical condition. Certain conditions increase the risk of kidney failure and these are as follows. If you are hospitalized for a serious condition that would require intensive care, age factor, blockages in blood vessels in your limbs, diabetes, kidney and/or liver diseases, heart diseases, and high blood pressure are leading causes.

COMMON CAUSES OF CKD IN CHILDREN

The diagnosis is made difficult by the number of diseases that can cause chronic kidney failure in children. Hence the importance of optimizing the detection and prevention of these diseases as soon as possible, there are three main responsible causes:

The diseases of the urinary system

Discovered during pregnancy or in the newborn, vesico-uretero-renal reflux is one of the most common reasons for the disease of the urinary tract, this disorder prevents urine from flowing normally, and makes it go up in the kidneys. There is a risk of progressive destruction of the kidneys over several decades. Other abnormalities of the urinary system diagnosed by ultrasound can also lead to kidney failure in children.

Hereditary diseases

These diseases can be the consequence of abnormal renal development and appear in the newborn. They may be responsible for the more or less long term, in the absence of appropriate management, severe kidney failure. There are also cystic diseases, the most representative of which is a recessive polycystic disease. Other glomerular or tubular disorders, such as nephrotic syndrome or Bartter syndrome, can lead to CKD, there is kidney damage associated with metabolic disorders such as cystinosis.

The diseases acquired during childhood

These diseases can be established acutely and severely, without warning, with, for example, the cases of acute glomerulonephritis whose evolution can lead to a CKR. The evolution can be done chronically; the most frequently encountered case is Berger's disease, which is often preceded by infectious episodes.

Elements That Come Into Play

- Evaluation of the nutritional state: the weight of form or health, current weight, loss/weight gain (attention to possible "demes") make it possible to evaluate the risk of malnutrition (Kondrup score) and therefore the intensity of dietary recommendations. More precise anthropometric measurements (skin folds, brachial muscular circumference) may complete this assessment.

- Food history: a complete assessment of the patient's eating habits is practiced judging the level of priority of the topics to be addressed, according to the medical prescription. The following are evaluated: caloric consumption, protein (animal/vegetable), phosphorus, salt, and potassium.

The diet will be adapted to the patient's tastes and habits to ensure optimal compliance in the medium term.

In young patients, food history often shows spontaneous protein intakes of more than 1.5 g/kg/day. The recommendation of 0.8 g/kg/day is very difficult to obtain in the long term. A progressive reduction of spontaneous contributions is then recommended, feasible in several stages. It generally concerns products of animal origin, which are widely consumed in Switzerland (meat, cheese). Older patients, on the other hand, readily have an insufficient spontaneous intake of calories and proteins, predisposing them to undernutrition. As a result, no diet should be prescribed. The equilibrium between animal sources (meat, fish, and eggs) of very good biological and vegetable value (cereals and derived products, potatoes, vegetables, and fruits) should tend towards a ratio of 50/50, even 60 / 40.

The recommended caloric intake is 30–35 kcal/kg/day, to be adjusted according to the age and activity level of the patient. They help to cover nutritional needs.

In some cases, much of the caloric intake can be provided by fat due to reduced protein intake and carbohydrate monitoring (diabetes). However, since patients also have a high cardiovascular risk, general public health recommendations are made on the choice of foods, especially fats. The criteria for a balanced diet must be respected (food pyramid of the Swiss Nutrition Society, Swiss Heart Foundation).

The fractionation of the diet makes it possible to palliate the lack of appetite, often described in the severe CRI, to guarantee satisfactory caloric contributions.

Luckily, foods high in phosphorus are often foods high in animal protein, which is recommended to reduce consumption.

However, foods with high phosphorus content such as milk, dairy products, especially cooked cheeses, must be quantified and spread over the week. The use of phosphorus-chelating drugs (and sources of calcium) should be considered quickly so that adequate intakes of protein and calcium can be maintained.

Limitation of dietary potassium intake is only considered in the severe stage of CKD and when serum potassium exceeds 5.5 mmol / l. Recommendations for food selection, daily and weekly distribution, and food preparation tips will complete the information.

The limitation of salt intake is only indicated in the case of arterial hypertension and/or edema. But, particular vigilance must be in order, because a low sodium diet is anorectic. Associated with other restrictions, the monotony of this diet will accelerate progress towards undernutrition. Advice on food choice and how to prepare it helps reduce dietary intake of salt.

Nutritional management of CKD needs to be nuanced. A moderate-protein diet of 0.8 g/kg/day can be proposed in patients who are undernourished, motivated, and supported by a multidisciplinary and experienced team providing periodic monitoring of nutritional status. A caloric intake of 30 to 35 kcal/d is necessary to limit significant morbidity and mortality related to under-nutrition.

Chronic renal failure in children is a delicate subject, above all for the child himself but also his family. Not being autonomous, his family and the medical profession need to redouble their vigilance to accompany him as best as possible and allow him to have a childhood as close to normal as possible.

LEARNING TO DEAL WITH KIDNEY FAILURE

Learning that you are suffering from kidney failure might be a difficult thing to cope with. No matter how long you have been preparing for the inevitable, this is something that will come as a shock to you.

But, as mentioned earlier, just because you have started dialysis, doesn't mean that everything that you hold dear has to come to an end!

It might be a little bit difficult at first to get yourself oriented to a new routine, but once you get into the groove, you'll start feeling much better.

Your nurses, loved ones, doctors, and co-workers will all be there to support you.

To make things easier, though, let me break down the individual types of problems that you might face and how you can deal with them.

Stress During Kidney Failure

When you are suffering from kidney failure, it's normal to be stressed out all the time. This might lead you to skip meals or even forget your medication, which might affect your health even more.

But you need to understand that life is full of hurdles and setbacks, and you really can't let them hold you back.

In that light, here are six tips to help you keep your stress under control:

1. Make sure to take some time to just relax and unwind. Try to practice deep breathing, visualization, meditation, or even muscle relaxation. All of these will help you to stay calm and keep your body healthy.

2. Make sure to involve yourself in regular exercise. Take a hike, ride a bicycle, or just simply take a jog. They all help. And if those aren't your thing, then you can always go for something more soothing, like tai chi or yoga.

3. When you are feeling too stressed, try to call up a friend or a beloved family member and talk to them. And if that's not helping, you can always take help from a psychiatrist/counselor.

4. Try to accept the things that are not under your control, and you can't change. Trying to enforce a change on something that is not within your reach will only make things worse for you. Better advice is to look for better ways of handling the situation instead of trying to change it.

5. Don't put too much pressure on yourself, try to be good to yourself, and don't expect much. You are a human being, after all, right? You can make mistakes, so accept that. Just try your best.

6. And lastly, always try to maintain a positive attitude. Even when things go completely wrong, try to see the good instead of the bad and focus on that. Try to find things in all phases of your life that make you happy and that you appreciate, such as your friends, work, health, and family, for example. You have no idea how much help a simple change of perspective can bring.

Exercise

Apart from the special diet, such as the Renal Diet, physical activity is another way through which you can improve the quality of your life.

This might be a little bit tough to do if you are alone, but it is very much possible. However, you should keep in mind that working out alone won't help you; you must work out and follow a well-balanced, healthy diet.

Both of these combined wills go to great lengths to help you lose weight and control your disease.

A study has shown that people who try to complete 10,1000 steps per day and work out for about 2½ hours every week, while cutting down 500–800 calories per day and following a proper diet routine, have a 50% chance of reducing blood sugar to normal levels, which will further help you to stay healthy.

Common forms of exercise include:

• Stair climbing

- Tai Chi

- Stretching

- Yoga

- Cycling

- Walking

- Swimming

To perform these normal workouts, you don't have to join a gym or even buy any sort of expensive equipment! You can simply take a walk around your streets; do yoga at home, and so on.

Just make sure to consult with your doctor to find out which exercise is suitable for you and adjust it to your dialysis routine.

Anxiety and Depression

These two are possibly the most prominent issues that you are going to face. A feeling of depression might last for a long time if left unattended. Anxiety might come at the same time, but it won't last for long.

Either way, mood swings will occur that will suddenly make you sad.

However, you should know that it is completely normal to feel anxious or sad when you're going through such a huge change in life. This is even more prominent if you start taking dialysis, as it will require you to completely change your daily routine and follow a different type of diet.

During this adjusting phase, you'll feel many emotions, such as anger, fear, sadness, etc.

To summarize, the symptoms of depression are:

- Loss of interest

- Loss of any appetite

- Sleeping problems

On the other hand, symptoms of anxiety are:

- Constant sweating

- Quick breathing

- Inconsistent heartbeat

- Constant troubling thoughts

Regardless, the main thing to know is that you are not alone in this fight. Thousands of people have and are going through the same experience. Many people often feel left alone and lose the will to fight, but it doesn't have to be the same for you.

Help is always available! Try sharing with your family members, join support groups, talk to a social worker, etc.

It doesn't matter what your situation is; if you just reach out to the right person, then you will always find the help and support that you need.

ANSWERS TO FREQUENTLY ASKED QUESTIONS

Below are some of the most common questions about CKD.

Are Sodas Bad For a Kidney?

When considering sodas, make sure that you avoid dark sodas, such as Pepsi or Coca Cola as they include phosphorus additives that are extremely harmful to your kidneys. Replace them with Cherry 7 Up, 7 Up, cream soda, ginger ale, sprite, etc. But even so, make sure to have them in very small amounts, as little as possible.

Is Cheese Allowed or Completely Forbidden?

As a rule of thumb, cheese should be avoided as it contains large amounts of phosphorus. However, some cheese is lower in phosphorus, such as cream cheese, Swiss Cheese, Natural Cheese, etc. One or two ounces of those once in a while won't hurt you.

What Are Some of the Precautions That I Can Take?

There are multiple steps that you can take to protect your kidneys. Some include:

- Follow a kidney-friendly diet, such as the renal diet

- Make sure to keep your blood pressure under control

- Stop smoking

- Keep your blood glucose level under check

Is There a Permanent Cure for CKD?

Unfortunately, no. Just like Asthma, once you get affected by CKD, you can only hope to keep it under check through proper management. There is no known permanent treatment at the moment.

What Are the Most Common Medications That I Should Avoid?

Some common medications to avoid that might lead to kidney diseases include:

- Over-the-counter painkillers
- Laxatives
- Enemas
- Anti-Inflammatory medicines
- Food supplements
- Vitamin and herbal medications

Always make sure to consult your Nephrologist before taking any over-the-counter medicine that might fall into any of the above categories.

What Are Some Common Tests to Assess Kidney Functions?

Some common tests to check the condition of your kidney include:

- Blood tests that specifically look for BUN, Electrolytes, and Serum Creatinine.
- Urine tests that check for Glomerular Filtration rate and Microalbumin.
- Imaging tests such as renal ultrasound, CT Scan, or MRI.
- Kidney biopsy, where a small part of your kidney is removed by a needle to know if it is affected.

SODIUM, POTASSIUM, AND PHOSPHOROUS ROLES IN OUR BODY

Sodium and its Role in the Body

Most natural foods contain sodium. Some people think that sodium and salt are interchangeable. However, salt is a compound of chloride and sodium. There might be either salt or sodium in other forms in the food we eat. Due to the added salt, processed foods include a higher level of sodium.

Apart from potassium and chloride, sodium is one of the most crucial body's electrolytes. The main function of electrolytes is controlling the fluids when they are going in and out of the body's cells and tissues.

Sodium helps your body with:

- Blood volume and pressure are regulated
- Muscle contraction and nerve function are regulated
- The acid-base balance of the blood is regulated
- The amount of fluid the body eliminates and keeps is balanced

Why is it important to monitor sodium intake for people with kidney issues?

Since the kidneys of kidney disease patients are unable to reduce excess fluid and sodium from the body adequately, too much sodium might be harmful. As fluid and sodium build up in the bloodstream and tissues, they might cause:

- Edema: swelling in face, hands, and legs
- Increased thirst
- High blood pressure
- Shortness of breath
- Heart failure

The ways to monitor sodium intake:

- Avoid processed foods
- Be attentive to serving sizes
- Read food labels
- Utilize fresh meats instead of processed
- Choose fresh fruits and veggies
- Compare brands, choosing the ones with the lowest sodium levels
- Utilize spices that do not include salt
- Ensure the sodium content is less than 400 mg per meal and not more than 150 mg per snack

- Cook at home, not adding salt

Foods to eat with lower sodium content:

- Fresh meats, dairy products, frozen veggies, and fruits

- Fresh herbs and seasonings like rosemary, oregano, dill, lime, cilantro, onion, lemon, and garlic

- Corn tortilla chips, pretzels, no salt added crackers, unsalted popcorn

A mineral that helps regulate your body's water content and blood pressure is sodium. Healthy kidneys can remove sodium from the body as needed, but when your kidneys do not work well, sodium can build up and can cause high blood pressure, fluid-weight gain, and thirst. High blood pressure increases the chance of your kidney disease getting worse. If you are in the early stages of chronic kidney disease (stages 1 to 4), you will need to make some dietary modifications if you have high blood pressure or if you are retaining fluid. If you are experiencing stage five chronic kidney disease and require dialysis, you will need to follow a low-sodium diet and not consume more than 1,500 milligrams of sodium each day, which is equivalent to a little less than 1 teaspoon of salt. (It is important to note 1 teaspoon of salt each day is the total amount of sodium you are allowed, which includes all foods plus added salt.) Follow a sodium-restricted diet carefully to keep your blood pressure under control. Controlling your blood pressure may also prevent your risk of developing heart disease and decrease the chances of your kidney disease getting worse.

Potassium and its Role in the Body

The main function of potassium is keeping muscles working correctly and the heartbeat regular. This mineral is responsible for maintaining electrolyte and fluid balance in the bloodstream. The kidneys regulate the proper amount of potassium in the body, expelling excess amounts in the urine.

- Monitoring potassium intake

- Limit high potassium food

- Select only fresh fruits and veggies

- Limit dairy products and milk to 8 oz per day

- Avoid potassium chloride

- Read labels on packaged foods

- Avoid seasonings and salt substitutes with potassium

You need potassium in your body to keep your heart strong and healthy. It is also needed to keep the water balance between your cells and body fluids in check. Healthy kidneys remove excess potassium through urination. The reason why kidneys are not functioning properly is they cannot remove the potassium, so it builds up in the blood.

While some people with kidney disease need more potassium, others need less. Depending on how well your kidneys are functioning, your potassium need may vary.

All foods contain some potassium, but some foods contain large amounts of potassium. On the following pages is a table that lists low-potassium, medium-potassium, and high-potassium foods. If you have chronic kidney disease, the amount of potassium you eat is not usually restricted unless your blood potassium level is high. Please talk with your physician about having your blood potassium level checked. And if you are receiving dialysis, your potassium intake should be kept between 2,000 and 3,000 milligrams per day.

Phosphorus and its Role in the Body

This mineral is essential in bone development and maintenance. Phosphorus helps in the development of connective organs and tissue and assists in muscle movement. Extra phosphorus is possible to be removed by healthy kidneys. However, it is impossible with kidney dysfunction. High levels of phosphorus make bones weak by pulling calcium out of your bones. It might lead to dangerous calcium deposits in the heart, eyes, lungs, and blood vessels.

Monitoring phosphorus intake

- Pay attention to serving size

- Eat fresh fruits and veggies

- Eat smaller portions of foods that are rich in protein

- Avoid packaged foods

- Keep a food journal

Foods to eat with low phosphorus levels:

- grapes, apples

- lettuce, leeks

- Carbohydrates (white rice, corn, and rice Cereal, popcorn, pasta, crackers (not wheat), white bread)

- Meat (sausage, fresh meat)

Phosphorus is a naturally occurring mineral. Phosphates are salt compounds containing phosphorus and other minerals, and these are found in our bones. Along with calcium, phosphorus helps build strong and healthy bones. Healthy kidneys can remove extra phosphorus in the blood. Virtually all foods have phosphorus or phosphate additives, so it is difficult to eliminate them from your diet.

If you have excess phosphorus in your blood, calcium is pulled from your bones, resulting in weak bones. When the kidneys are failing, phosphorus builds up in the blood and may cause problems such as severe itching, muscle aches and pain, bone disease, and hardening of the blood vessels, including those leading to the heart, as well as deposits on the skin and in the joints.

The table on the following pages lists low-phosphorus, medium-phosphorus, and high-phosphorus foods. Please talk with your physician about getting your blood phosphorus level checked.

UNDERSTANDING RENAL DIET

A proper diet is necessary for controlling the amount of toxic waste in the bloodstream. When toxic waste piles up in the system along with increased fluid, chronic inflammation occurs and we will be more prone to having cardiovascular, bone, metabolic, or other health issues.

Since your kidneys can't fully get rid of the waste on their own, which comes from food and drinks, probably the only natural way to help our system is through this diet.

A renal diet is especially useful during the first stages of kidney dysfunction and leads to the following benefits:

- Prevents excess fluid and waste build-up

- Prevents the progression of renal dysfunction stages

- Decreases the likelihood of developing other chronic health problems e.g. heart disorders

- Has a mild antioxidant function in the body, which keeps inflammation and inflammatory responses under control.

The above-mentioned benefits are noticeable once the patient follows the diet for at least a month and then continues it for longer periods to avoid the stage where dialysis is needed. The strictness of the diet depends on the current stage of renal/kidney disease, if, for example, you are in the 3rd or 4th stage, you should follow a stricter diet and be attentive to the food, which is allowed or prohibited.

Doctors and dietitians have developed a diet that helps their patients with compromised kidney function cut down the amount of waste that their body produces that their kidneys can't filter out. A renal diet is lower in sodium, phosphorus, and protein than a typical diet. Every person's body is different, which means that what works for one person will not work for another. Some people have to cut their levels of potassium and calcium as well. A renal diet must be tailored to meet the individual needs and toxin levels of the patient. Keeping a food journal may become necessary and is highly recommended. Sometimes it can be hard to keep track of all of the foods and their amounts; a journal can make keeping track a lot less intimidating. A physical notebook or even a cell phone application can be used for this.

SODIUM (MG)

Sodium and table salt are two different components. Table salt is comprised of sodium and chloride. However, sodium by itself is a mineral that is naturally occurring in most of the foods that we eat. That is the reason why processed foods are not recommended for someone with kidney problems or in a renal diet due to the added salt that is put into them. Sodium is one of three major electrolytes that help control the fluids going in and out of the cells and tissue in the body. Sodium is responsible for helping control blood pressure and volume, muscle contraction and nerve functions, regulating the acid and base balance of the blood, and balancing the elimination and retention of fluid in the body.

Renal patients are required to monitor their sodium intake because when the kidney's functions become compromised, it is harder for their body to eliminate the fluids and the sodium that is in excess in the body. It has side effects that include:

- Increased thirst

- Edema

- High blood pressure

- Shortness of breath from the fluid being retained in the lungs

- Heart failure from an overworked and weak heart that has had to work harder due to the body making it work harder

Limiting sodium can be easier than you think. Since sodium content is always listed on food labels, it is important to get into the habit of checking not only sodium content but the single serving size as well. As a rule of thumb, fresh is better. Packaged foods typically have added salt, so stick with things that have no salt added to them. Start comparing the items you use. If it is a spice, steer clear of something with "salt" in the title. When you are cooking in your home, do not add extra salt to your food under any circumstance. Too much sodium can make chronic kidney disease progress much faster.

POTASSIUM (MG)

Potassium is another of the three major electrolytes in the body. It is a naturally occurring mineral found in many foods and our bodies. Potassium helps keep our hearts beating regularly and our muscles working correctly. The kidneys have a duty when regulating the amount of potassium in the body. These organs, when healthy, know just how much potassium your body needs. Excess potassium is cleansed from the body through the body's urine output. When you have chronic kidney disease, this naturally occurring regulation in the body becomes compromised.

Hyperkalemia, come with the following symptoms:

- Weakness in the muscles

- Irregular heartbeat

- A pulse that is slower than normal

- Heart attack/Stroke

- Death

Learning how to limit potassium, just like sodium, is an important part of your renal diet. Foods like bananas, fish, spinach, avocados, and potatoes are high in potassium and are foods to avoid. Cut down on your milk and dairy consumption to eight ounces per day. Make sure to read the labels and adhere to the single serving size of the foods you are eating.

PHOSPHORUS (MG)

Phosphorus is a mineral that aids the bones and the muscles in the body. When food is ingested, the small intestines absorb the amount of phosphorus needed for the bones, but the kidneys are in charge of removing the extra phosphorus. When the kidneys can't expel the extra phosphorus, it builds up in the blood and pulls calcium from the bones, making them weak. High amounts of phosphorus can also cause calcium deposits to build up in the heart, lungs, eyes, and blood vessels.

Keeping phosphorus levels low, just like sodium and potassium, are important in a renal diet. Stop eating foods that are rich in phosphorus like soda, cheese, meat, milk, and seeds. It may be necessary to discuss using phosphate binders with your doctor to keep your levels under control. Make sure to avoid foods with added phosphorus. These will be labeled with "PHOS" on the label.

PROTEIN (G)

Protein levels can be a tricky thing to keep equaled out if you have chronic kidney disease. Different stages of CKD tolerate protein levels differently and depending on which stage of CKD you are experiencing; your diet will reflect a different level of proteins allowed. Proteins are important to the body, so you can't eliminate them from your diet. You can be aware of your intake and what your body can tolerate and what it can't.

Fluid intake needs to be strictly monitored due to the probability of the fluid being retained in the body. When a person is on dialysis, their urine output is decreased, so extra fluid can cause unnecessary strain on the body. Fluid intake levels will be calculated by a nutritionist or doctor on a personal basis. Never drink more than what the doctor tells you is okay, and do not forget to consider solids that turn to liquid at room temperature or used in cooking.

How to Slow Kidney Disease

A kidney disease diagnosis can seem devastating at first. The news may come as a shock for some people, who may not have experienced any symptoms. It's important to remember that you can control your progress and improvement through diet and lifestyle changes, even when a prognosis is serious. Taking steps to improve your health can make a significant effort to slow the progression of kidney disease and improve your quality of life.

1. Focus on Weight Loss

Losing weight is one of the most common reasons for going on a diet. It's also one of the best ways to treat kidney disease and prevent further damage. Carrying excess weight contributes to high toxicity levels in the body, by storing toxins instead of releasing them through the kidneys.

Eating foods high in trans fats, sugar, and excess sodium contribute to obesity, which affects close to one-third of North Americans and continues to rise in many other countries, where fast foods are becoming easier to access and less expensive. Losing weight is a difficult cycle for many, who often diet temporarily only to return to unhealthy habits after reaching a milestone, which results in gaining the weight back, thus causing an unhealthy "yo-yo" diet effect.

There are some basic and easy changes you can make to shed those first pounds, which will begin to take the pressure off the kidneys and help you onto the path of regular weight loss:

- Drink plenty of water. If you can't drink eight glasses a day, try adding unsweetened natural sparkling water or herbal teas to increase your water intake.

- Reduce the amount of sugar and carbohydrates you consume. This doesn't require adapting to a ketogenic or low-carb diet—you'll notice a major change after ditching soda and reducing the bread and pasta by half.

- Take your time to eat and avoid rushing. If you need to eat in a hurry, grab a piece of fruit or a small portion of macadamia nuts. Avoid sugary and salty foods as much as possible. Choose fresh fruits over potato chips and chocolate bars.

- Create a shortlist of kidney-friendly foods that you enjoy and use this as your reference or guide when grocery shopping. This will help you stock up on snacks, ingredients, and foods for your kitchen that work well within your renal diet plan, at the same time reducing your chances of succumbing to the temptation of eating a bag of salted pretzels or chocolate.

Once you make take a few steps towards changing the way you eat, it will get easier. Making small changes at first is the key to success and to progressing with a new way of eating and living. If you are already in the habit of consuming packaged foods—such as crackers, chips, processed dips, sauces, and sodas—try cutting down on one or two items at a time, and over a while, gradually eliminate and cut down other items. Slowly replace these with fresh foods and healthier choices, so that your body has a chance to adapt without extreme cravings that often occur during sudden changes.

2. Quit Smoking and Reduce Alcohol

It's not easy to quit smoking or using recreational drugs, especially where there has been long-term use and the effects have already made an impact on your health. At some point, you'll begin to notice a difference in the way you feel and how your body changes over time. This includes chronic coughing related to respiratory conditions, shortness of breath, and a lack of energy. These changes may be subtle at first, and it may appear as though there is minimal damage or none at all, though smoking inevitably catches up with age and contributes to the development of cancer, premature aging, and kidney damage. The more toxins we consume or add to our body, the more challenging it becomes for the kidneys to work efficiently, which eventually slows their ability to function.

For most people, quitting "cold turkey" or all at once is not an option, because of the withdrawal symptoms and increased chances of starting again. This method, however, can work if applied with a strong support system and a lot of determination, though it's not the best option for everyone. Reducing smoking on your own, or switching to e-cigarettes or a patch or medication, can help significantly over time. Setting goals of reduction until the point of quitting can be a beneficial way to visualize success and provide a sense of motivation.

The following tips may also be useful for quitting smoking and other habit-forming substances:

- Join a support group and talk to other people who relate to you. Share your struggles, ideas, and thoughts, which will help others as well as yourself during this process.

- Track your progress on a calendar or in a notebook, either by pen and paper or on an application. This can serve as a motivator, as well as a means to display how you've done so far and where you can improve. For example, you may have reduced your smoking from ten to seven cigarettes per day, then increased to nine. This may indicate a slight change that can keep in mind to focus on reducing your intake further, from nine cigarettes to seven or six per day, and so on.

- Be aware of stressors in your life that cause you to smoke or use substances. If these factors are avoidable, make every effort to minimize or stop them from impacting your life. This may include specific people, places, or situations that can "trigger" a craving or make you feel more likely to use it than usual. If there are situations that you cannot avoid, such as family, work, or school-related situations, consult with a trusted friend or someone you can confide in who can be present with you during these instances.

- Don't be afraid to ask for help. Many people cannot quit on their own without at least some assistance from others. Seeking the guidance and expertise of a counselor or medical professional to better yourself can be one of the most important decisions you make to improve the quality of your life.

3. Getting Active

One of the most important ways to keep fit and healthy is by staying active and engaging in regular exercise. Regular movement is key, and exercise is different for everyone, depending on their abilities and options available. Fortunately, there are unlimited ways to customize an exercise routine or plan that can suit any lifestyle, perhaps low impact to start, or if you're ready, engage in a more vigorous workout. For many people experiencing kidney disease, one of the major struggles is losing weight and living a sedentary life, where movement is generally minimal, and exercise is generally not practiced. Smoking, eating processed foods, and not getting the required nutrition can further impair the body in such a way that exercise is seen as a hurdle and a challenge that is best avoided. Making lifestyle changes is not something that should be done all at once, but over a while—especially during the early stages of renal disease—so that the impact of the condition is minimized over time and becomes more manageable.

Where can you begin, if you haven't exercised at all or for a long period? For starters, don't sign up for a marathon or engage in any strenuous activities unless it is safe to do so. Start slow and take your time. Before taking on any new movements—whether it is minimal, low-impact walking or stretching, or a more moderate to high-impact regimen—always talk to your doctor to rule out any impact this may have on other existing conditions, such as blood pressure and respiratory conditions, as well as your kidneys. Most, if not all, physicians will likely recommend exercise as part of the treatment plan but may advise beginning slowly if your body isn't used to exercise.

Simple techniques to introduce exercise into your life require a commitment. This can begin with a quick 15-minute walk or jog and a 10- or 15-minute stretch in the morning before starting your day.

There are several easy, introductory techniques to consider, including the following:

- Take a walk for 10 to 15 minutes each day, at least three or four days each week. If you find it difficult at first, due to cramping, respiratory issues, or other conditions, walk slowly and breathe deeply. Make sure you feel relaxed during your walks. Find a scenic path or area in your neighborhood that is pleasant and gives you something to enjoy, such as a beautiful sunset or forested park. Bring a bottle of water to keep yourself hydrated.

- Stretch for five minutes once a day. This doesn't mean you need to do any intricate yoga poses or specific techniques. Moving your ankles, wrists, and arms in circles and standing every so often (if you sit often), and twisting your torso can help release stress and improve your blood flow, which lowers blood pressure and helps your body transport nutrients to areas in need of repair.

- Practice breathing long, measured breaths. This will help prepare you for more endurance-based exercise, such as jogging, long walks, cycling, and swimming. Count to five on each inhale and exhale, and practice moving slowly as you breathe, to "sync" or coordinate your body's movements with your breathing. If you have difficulty with the respiratory system, take it slow and don't push yourself. If you feel weak or out of breath, stop immediately and try again later or the next day at a slower pace.

- Start a beginner's yoga class and learn the fundamentals of various poses and stretches. It is helpful to arrive early and speak with the instructor, who can provide guidance on which modifications work best if needed. They may also be able to provide tips on how to approach certain poses or movements that can be challenging for beginners so that you feel more comfortable and knowledgeable before you start.

If you smoke, exercise will present more of a challenge to your lungs and respiratory function. Once you become accustomed to a beginner's level and become moderately active, you may notice it takes more effort, which requires an increase in lung capacity and oxygen. Smoking will eventually present a challenge, and where quitting can be a long-term and difficult goal in itself, make an effort to cut back as much as it takes to allow your body's movements and exercise to continue. In time, you may find quitting becomes easier and more achievable than expected!

Once you get into a basic routine, there is a wide variety of individual and team activities to consider for your life. If you are a social person, joining a baseball team or badminton club may be ideal. For more solitary options, consider swimming, cycling, or jogging. Many gyms and community centers provide monthly plans and may offer a free trial period to see if their facilities work for you. This is a great opportunity to try new classes and equipment to gauge how much you can achieve, even if in the early stages of exercise so that you can decide whether to pursue dance aerobics, spin classes, and/or weight training. Some gyms will provide a free consultation with a personal trainer to set a simple plan for weight loss and strength training goals.

Volume

Imperial	Metric		Imperial	Metric
1 tbsp	15ml		1 pint	570 ml
2 fl oz	55 ml		1 ¼ pints	725 ml
3 fl oz	75 ml		1 ¾ pints	1 litre
5 fl oz (¼ pint)	150 ml		2 pints	1.2 litres
10 fl oz (½ pint)	275 ml		2½ pints	1.5 litres
			4 pints	2.25 litres

Weight

Imperial	Metric		Imperial	Metric		Imperial	Metric
½ oz	10 g		4 oz	110 g		10 oz	275 g
¾ oz	20 g		4½ oz	125 g		12 oz	350 g
1 oz	25 g		5 oz	150 g		1 lb	450 g
1½ oz	40 g		6 oz	175 g		1 lb 8 oz	700 g
2 oz	50 g		7 oz	200 g		2 lb	900 g
2½ oz	60 g		8 oz	225 g		3 lb	1.35 kg
3 oz	75 g		9 oz	250 g			

Metric cups conversion

Cups	Imperial	Metric
1 cup flour	5oz	150g
1 cup caster or granulated sugar	8oz	225g
1 cup soft brown sugar	6oz	175g
1 cup soft butter/margarine	8oz	225g
1 cup sultanas/raisins	7oz	200g
1 cup currants	5oz	150g
1 cup ground almonds	4oz	110g
1 cup oats	4oz	110g
1 cup golden syrup/honey	12oz	350g
1 cup uncooked rice	7oz	200g
1 cup grated cheese	4oz	110g
1 stick butter	4oz	110g
¼ cup liquid (water, milk, oil, etc)	4 tablespoons	60ml
½ cup liquid (water, milk, oil, etc)	¼ pint	125ml
1 cup liquid (water, milk, oil, etc)	½ pint	250ml

Oven temperatures

Gas Mark	Fahrenheit	Celsius	Gas Mark	Fahrenheit	Celsius
1/4	225	110	4	350	180
1/2	250	130	5	375	190
1	275	140	6	400	200
2	300	150	7	425	220
3	325	170	8	450	230
			9	475	240

Oven temperatures

Gas Mark	Fahrenheit	Celsius	Gas Mark	Fahrenheit	Celsius
1/4	225	110	4	350	180
1/2	250	130	5	375	190
1	275	140	6	400	200
2	300	150	7	425	220
3	325	170	8	450	230
			9	475	240

Weight

Imperial	Metric	Imperial	Metric
½ oz	10 g	6 oz	175 g
¾ oz	20 g	7 oz	200 g
1 oz	25 g	8 oz	225 g
1½ oz	40 g	9 oz	250 g
2 oz	50 g	10 oz	275 g
2½ oz	60 g	12 oz	350 g
3 oz	75 g	1 lb	450 g
4 oz	110 g	1 lb 8 oz	700 g
4½ oz	125 g	2 lb	900 g
5 oz	150 g	3 lb	1.35 kg

Chapter 2

Breakfast Recipes

APPLE MUFFINS

Preparation Time: 10 minutes

Cooking time: 12 minutes

Serving:4

Ingredients:

4 tablespoons wheat flour

2 apples, peeled

1 tablespoon soy yogurt

½ teaspoon baking powder

¼ teaspoon lemon juice

1 teaspoon vanilla extract

Directions:

1. Cook the apples until soft and place them in a blender. Pulse until pure.
2. Then combine apple pure with flour, yogurt, baking powder, and lemon juice.
3. Add vanilla extract and stir the batter until smooth.
4. Fill ½ part of every muffin mold with batter and bake them for 12 minutes at 365F.
5. Chill the muffins and remove them from the muffin molds.

Nutrition:

- Calories 87,
- Fat 0.3 g
- Fiber 1.8 g
- Carbs 20.2 g
- Protein 1.7 g

CITRUS BLUEBERRY MUFFINS

Preparation time: 5 minutes

Cooking time:30 minutes

Serving:4

Ingredients:

2 cups blueberries

2 tsp. phosphorus-free baking powder

1 tsp. lime zest

2 cups plain flour

1/2 cup light sour cream

1 tsp. lemon zest

1 cup unsweetened rice milk

2 eggs

1 cup sugar

1/2 cup melted coconut oil

Directions:

1. Warm the oven to 400 F. Take a cupcake tin and place paper liners in each cup.
2. Place the sugar and coconut oil into a medium bowl. Using a hand mixer, beat until fluffy.
3. Add in sour cream, rice milk, and eggs.
4. Scrape and continue to mix until well blended.
5. Add baking powder, lime zest, lemon zest, and flour to a small bowl. Stir together to combine.
6. Mix the flour mixture into the eggs until it just comes together. Add in the blueberries and stir again.
7. Spoon into prepared muffin papers. Don't overfill.
8. Place into the preheated oven and bake for 25 minutes.
9. Check to make sure a toothpick comes out clean when stuck to the muffins. Serve and enjoy!

Nutrition:

- Calories: 252
- Protein: 4 g
- Sodium: 26 mg
- Potassium: 107 mg
- Phosphorus: 79 mg

MILLET MUFFINS

Preparation time: 10 minutes

Cooking time: 15 minutes

Serving: 12

Ingredients:

¼ cup coconut oil, melted

1 egg

½ teaspoon vanilla extract

1 teaspoon baking powder

1½ cups organic millet, cooked

½ cup coconut sugar

Cooking spray

Directions:

1. In a blender, blend the melted coconut oil with the egg, vanilla extract, baking powder, millet, and sugar. Grease a muffin tray with cooking spray and divide the millet mix into each cup. Place the muffins in the oven and bake at 350 degrees F for 30 minutes. Let the muffins cool and then serve!

2. Enjoy!

Nutrition:

- Calories 167,
- Fat 4,
- Fiber 7,
- Carbs 15,
- Protein 6

OATMEAL BERRY MUFFINS

Preparation time: 5 minutes

Cooking time: 30 minutes

Serving: 12

Ingredients:

½ cup quick-cooking oatmeal

1 cup unbleached all-purpose flour

½ tsp baking soda

⅔ cup lightly packed brown sugar

½ cup applesauce

2 eggs

Zest of 1 orange

¼ cup canola oil

1 tbsp lemon juice

Zest of 1 lemon

¾ cup blueberries, fresh or frozen

¾ cup raspberries, fresh or frozen

Directions:

1. Preheat the oven to 350°F. Line 12 muffin cups.
2. Combine baking soda, brown sugar, oatmeal, and flour in a bowl. Set aside.
3. Whisk lemon juice, applesauce, and eggs in a large bowl.
4. Stir in the dry ingredients with a wooden spoon.
5. Add the berries. Stir gently.
6. Scoop into the muffin cups.
7. Bake for 21 minutes. Let cool.

Nutrition:

- Protein - 2.8g
- Carbohydrates - 28g
- Fat - 5.9g
- Calories - 173

ZUCCHINI APPLE MUFFINS

Preparation time: 10 minutes

Cooking time: 20 minutes

Serving: 2

Ingredients:

1/2 cup diced cored and peeled apple

1 tsp. vanilla

1 egg

1/4 cup olive oil

1/4 cup honey

1 cup zucchini puree

2 tsp. Phosphorus=free baking powder

1 cup wheat bran

1 cup plain flour

Directions:

1. Warm the oven to 350 F. Take a cupcake tin and place a paper liner into each cup.

2. Add baking powder, wheat bran, and flour into a medium bowl. Stir to mix well.
3. Add the vanilla, egg, olive oil, honey, and zucchini to a small bowl and combine.
4. Mix the zucchini mixture into the dry ingredients.
5. Add in the apple and stir to combine.
6. Spoon batter into muffin papers. Don't overfill.
7. Bake for 20 minutes. Once over, stick a toothpick in the middle. If it comes out clean, it means they are done. Serve and enjoy!

Nutrition:
- Calories: 125
- Protein: 2 g
- Sodium: 8 mg
- Potassium: 177 mg
- Phosphorus: 120 mg

RHUBARB MUFFINS

Preparation time: 10 minutes

Cooking time: 25 minutes

Serving: 8

Ingredients:

½ cup almond meal

2 tablespoons crystallized ginger

¼ cup coconut sugar

1 tablespoon linseed meal

½ cup buckwheat flour

¼ cup rice flour

2 tablespoons powdered arrowroot

2 teaspoon gluten-free baking powder

½ teaspoon fresh grated ginger

½ teaspoon ground cinnamon

1 cup rhubarb, sliced

1 apple, cored, peeled, and chopped

1/3 cup almond milk, unsweetened

¼ cup olive oil

1 free-range egg

1 teaspoon vanilla extract

Directions:

1. In a bowl, mix the almond meal with the crystallized ginger, sugar, linseed meal, buckwheat flour, rice flour, arrowroot powder, grated ginger, baking powder, and cinnamon and stir

2. . In another bowl, mix the rhubarb with the apple, almond milk, oil, egg, and vanilla and stir well.

3. Combine the 2 mixtures, stir well, and divide into a lined muffin tray.

4. Place in the oven at 350 degrees F and bake for 25 minutes. Serve the muffins for breakfast.

5. Enjoy!

Nutrition:

- Calories 200
- Fat 4 g
- Fiber 6 g
- Carbs 13 g
- Protein 8 g

BREAKFAST CREPES

Preparation time: 10 minutes

Cooking time: 10 minutes

Serving: 4

Ingredients:

2 eggs

1 teaspoon vanilla extract

½ cup almond milk, unsweetened

½ cup water

2 tablespoons agave nectar

1 cup coconut flour

3 tablespoons coconut oil, melted

Directions:

1. In a bowl, whisk the eggs with the vanilla extract, almond milk, water, and agave nectar. Add the flour and 2 tablespoons oil gradually and stir until you obtain a smooth batter.
2. Heat a pan with the rest of the oil over medium heat, add some of the batter, spread it into the pan, and cook the crepe until it's golden on both sides then transfer to a plate. Repeat with the rest of the batter and serve the crepes for breakfast.
3. Enjoy!

Nutrition:

- Calories 121
- Fat 3 g
- Fiber 6 g
- Carbs 14 g
- Protein 6 **g**

OATMEAL PANCAKES

Preparation time: 5 minutes

Cooking time:30 minutes

Serving:4

Ingredients:

1 tbsp. unsalted butter, divided

1 egg

1/2 cup unsweetened rice milk

Ground cinnamon, to taste

1/4 cup rolled oats

1 cup plain flour

Directions:

1. Put cinnamon, oats, and flour into a medium bowl and stir well to combine.
2. Add the egg and milk to the same bowl. Whisk together.
3. Add this to the flour mixture and whisk well to combine.

4. On a large skillet over medium heat, melt the butter.

5. Take .25 cup of the batter and pour it into the skillet.

6. Cook the pancake until the edges are firm and there are bubbles on the surface. This should take about 3 minutes.

7. Flip the pancake and cook until golden brown on this side. This will take around 2 more minutes.

8. Continue with the rest of the batter until it is completely used. Add butter to skillet as needed.

9. Serve pancakes hot. Enjoy!

Nutrition:

- Calories: 195
- Protein: 6 g
- Sodium: 60 mg
- Potassium: 92 mg
- Phosphorus: 109 mg

STRAWBERRY TOPPED WAFFLES

Preparation time: 5 minutes

Cooking time:40 minutes

Serving:4

Ingredients:

1 cup flour

1/4 cup Swerve

1 ¾ teaspoons baking powder

1 egg, separated

¾ cup milk

½ cup butter, melted

½ teaspoon vanilla extract

Fresh strawberries, sliced

Directions:

1. Prepare and preheat your waffle pan following the directions of the machine.

2. Begin by mixing the flour with Swerve and baking soda in a bowl.

3. Separate the egg yolks from the egg whites, keeping them in two separate bowls.
4. Add the milk and vanilla extract to the egg yolks.
5. Stir the melted butter and mix well until smooth.
6. Now beat the egg whites with an electric beater until foamy and fluffy.
7. Fold this fluffy composition in the egg yolk mixture.
8. Mix it gently until smooth, then add in the flour mixture.
9. Stir again to make a smooth mixture.
10. Pour a half cup of the waffle batter into a preheated pan and cook until the waffle is done.
11. Cook more waffles with the remaining batter.
12. Serve fresh with strawberries on top.

Nutrition:

- Calories 342,
- Total Fat 20.5g
- Saturated Fat 12.5g
- Cholesterol 88mg
- Sodium 156mg
- Carbohydrate 21g
- Dietary Fiber 0.7g
- Sugars 3.5g
- Protein 4.8g
- Calcium 107mg
- Phosphorous 126mg
- Potassium 233mg

GINGERBREAD OATMEAL

Preparation time: 10 minutes

Cooking time: 15 minutes

Serving: 4

Ingredients:

1 cup steel-cut oats

4 cups water

¼ teaspoon ground coriander

1½ tablespoons ground cinnamon

¼ teaspoon ground cloves

¼ teaspoon fresh grated ginger

¼ teaspoon ground allspice

¼ teaspoon ground cardamom

A pinch of ground nutmeg

Directions:

1. Heat a pan with the water over medium-high heat, add the oats, and stir. Add the coriander, cinnamon, cloves, ginger, allspice, cardamom, and nutmeg, stir, cook for 15 minutes, divide into bowls and serve.

2. Enjoy!

Nutrition:

- Calories 188
- Fat 3 g
- Fiber 6 g
- Carbs 13 g
- Protein 6 g

FETA AND BELL PEPPER QUICHE

Preparation time: 10 minutes

Cooking time: 20 minutes

Serving: 2

Ingredients:

Pepper, to taste

2 tbsp. chopped basil

1/4 cup low sodium feta cheese

1/4 cup plain flour

4 eggs

1 cup unsweetened rice milk

1 chopped bell pepper

1 tsp. minced garlic

1 small chopped sweet onion

1 tsp. olive oil plus more

Directions:

1. Warm your oven to 400 F. Brush a small amount of olive oil into a 9-inch pie pan.
2. Warm the oil in a skillet on medium heat.
3. Cook the onion and garlic until they become soft.
4. Add in bell pepper and cook for another 3 minutes.
5. Place the vegetables into the pie plate that has been brushed with olive oil.
6. Place the eggs, flour, and rice milk in a medium bowl and combine until smooth.
7. Add in the basil and feta, then sprinkle with pepper. Stir well to combine.
8. Pour eggs over the vegetables in the pie plate.
9. Bake until the edges are golden brown, and the center is just set. This should take about 20 minutes.
10. This can be served cold, room temperature, or hot. Enjoy!

Nutrition:

- Calories: 172
- Protein: 8 g
- Sodium: 154 mg
- Potassium: 122 mg
- Phosphorus: 120 mg

COURGETTE BASIL QUICHE

Preparation time: 5 minutes

Cooking time: 40 minutes

Serving: 4

Ingredients:

Pepper, to taste

1 tbsp. all-purpose flour

Minced garlic clove, to taste

1/2 cup crumbled feta

1 cup unsweetened rice milk

2 tbsp. chopped basil

3 eggs, beaten

2 chopped scallions

Chopped cabbage, to taste

2 cup finely chopped Courgettes

1 frozen pie crust

Directions:

1. Turn your oven to 425 F.
2. Lay the pie crust out into a pan and use a fork to pierce the crust in a few places so that it doesn't rise too much.
3. Allow the crust to bake for about 10 minutes.
4. Remove and lower the temperature of the oven to 325° F.
5. In a medium bowl, combine the flour, garlic, feta, rice milk, basil, eggs, scallions, cabbage, and courgettes. Sprinkle in some pepper.
6. Pour the egg mixture into the pie crust. Allow this to bake for 35 to 45 minutes. When you insert a knife in the center, it should come out clean.
7. Allow the quiche to cool for 10 to 15 minutes before you serve. Enjoy!

Nutrition:

*   Calories: 160
*   Protein: 6 g
*   Sodium: 259 mg
*   Potassium: 173 mg
*   Phosphorus: 101 mg

EGG DROP SOUP

Preparation time: 5 minutes

Cooking time: 10 minutes

Serving: 4

Ingredients:

¼ cup minced fresh chives

4 cups unsalted vegetable stock

4 whisked eggs

Directions:

1. Pour unsalted vegetable stock into the oven set over high heat. Bring to a boil. Turn down heat to the lowest heat setting.

2. Pour in the eggs. Stir continuously until ribbons form into the soup.

3. Turn off the heat immediately. The residual heat will cook eggs through.

4. Cool slightly before ladling the desired amount into individual bowls. Garnish with a pinch of parsley, if using. Serve immediately.

Nutrition:

- Calories 32
- Carbs 0 g
- Fat 2 g
- Protein 5.57 g
- Potassium (K) 67 mg
- Sodium (Na) 63 mg
- Phosphorus 36.1 mg

SUMMER SQUASH AND APPLE SOUP

Preparation time:10 minutes

Cooking time:40 minutes

Serving:4

Ingredients:

1 cup non-dairy milk

½ tsp. cumin

3 cups unsalted vegetable broth

1 ½ tsps. Grated ginger

1 tbsp. olive oil

1 lb. peeled summer squash

2 diced apples

¾ tsp. curry powder

Directions:

1. Set the oven to 375 °F.

2. Cut out a sheet of aluminum foil that is big enough to wrap the summer squash. Once wrapped, bake for 30 minutes.

3. Remove the wrapped summer squash from the oven and set aside to cool.

4. Once cooled, remove the aluminum foil, remove the seeds, and peel.

5. Dice the summer squash, then place in a food processor. Add non-dairy milk. Blend until smooth. Transfer to a bowl and set aside.

6. Place a soup pot over medium flame and heat through. Once hot, add the olive oil and swirl to coat.

7. Sauté the onion until tender, then add the diced apple, spices, and broth. Bring to a boil. Once boiling, reduce to a simmer and let simmer for about 8 minutes.

8. Turn off the heat and let cool slightly. Once cooled, pour the mixture into the food processor and blend until smooth.

9. Pour the pureed apple mixture back into the pot, then stir in the summer squash mixture. Mix well, then reheat to a simmer over medium flame. Serve.

Nutrition:

- Calories 240
- Protein 2.24g
- Potassium (K) 376 mg
- Sodium (Na) 429 mg
- Fat 8g, Carbs 40g
- Phosphorus 0g

ROASTED PEPPER SOUP

Preparation time:10 minutes

Cooking time:30 minutes

Serving:4

Ingredients:

2 cups unsalted vegetable broth

½ cup chopped carrots

2 large red peppers

¼ cup julienned sweet basil

2 minced garlic cloves

½ cup chopped celery

2 tbsps. Olive oil

½ cup chopped onion

½ cup almond milk

Directions:

1. Place the oven into the 375°F.
2. Put onions on a baking sheet. Add the red peppers beside the mixture. Drizzle some of the olive oil over everything and toss well to coat.
3. Roast for 20 minutes, or until peppers are tender and skins are wilted.
4. Chop the roasted red peppers and set aside.
5. Place a pot over medium-high flame and heat through. Once hot, add the olive oil and swirl to coat.
6. Place the carrot, celery, and garlic into the pot and sauté until carrot and celery are tender. Add the chopped roasted red peppers. Mix well.
7. Pour in the vegetable broth and almond milk. Increase to high flame and bring to a boil.
8. Once boiling, reduce to a simmer. Simmer, uncovered, for 10 minutes.
9. Turn off the heat and allow to cool slightly.
10. If desired, blend the soup using an immersion blender until the soup has reached a desired level of smoothness. Reheat over medium flame.
11. Add the basil and stir to combine. Serve.

Nutrition:

Calories 320

Protein 1.3g

Potassium (K) 249 mg

Sodium (Na) 45 mg

Fat 25g, Carbs 20g

Phosphorus 66.33 g

CHICKEN CONGEE

Preparation time: 5 minutes

Cooking time: 30 minutes

Serving: 4

Ingredients:

6 cups water

¼ cup brown or red rice, rinsed, drained

¼ cup frozen corn, thawed, drained

2 garlic cloves, grated

1 shallot, minced

1 thumb-sized ginger, peeled

1 tablespoon coconut oil

1 tablespoon low-sodium teriyaki sauce

½ pound chicken thigh fillets

Pinch of sea salt

Pinch of black pepper to taste

⅛ cup fresh cilantro, minced

Dash of garlic flakes

Directions:

1. Pour oil into a nonstick skillet set over medium heat. Sauté garlic and shallots until limp and aromatic; add in chicken. Stir-fry until meat browns; pour into a slow cooker set at medium heat.

2. Except for garnishes, pour in remaining ingredients; stir. Put a lid on. Cook for 6 hours. Turn off the heat. Fish out and discard ginger. Taste; adjust seasoning if needed.

3. Ladle congee into individual bowls. Garnish with equal portions of cilantro and garlic flakes. Serve with a wedge of lime. Squeeze lime juice over congee.

Nutrition:
- Protein 10.11g (19%),
- Potassium (K) 364 mg (8 %)
- Sodium (Na) 180 mg (12%)

QUINOA CONGEE WITH CAULIFLOWER

Preparation time: 5 minutes

Cooking time:20 minutes

Serving:4

Ingredients:

6 cups water

¼ cup quinoa

4 large leeks, minced, reserve green stems for garnish

1 small cauliflower head, minced

1 can mackerel in water, low-sodium, include liquid, flaked

1 tablespoon fresh ginger, grated

1 tablespoon low-sodium teriyaki sauce, add more later only if needed

¼ pound frozen scallops, thawed

½ pound frozen shrimps, thawed

Pinch of sea salt

Pinch of white pepper

1 lime, sliced into wedges

Directions:
1. Except for lime, scallops, and shrimps, pour the remaining ingredients into a slow cooker set at low heat. Stir. Put a lid on. Cook for 6 hours. Stir in scallops and shrimps; cook for another 15 minutes. Turn off the heat. Taste: adjust seasoning if needed.
2. Ladle congee into individual bowls. Garnish with leeks. Serve with a wedge of lime on the side. Squeeze lime juice into congee just before eating.

Nutrition:

- Protein 10.11g (19%)
- Potassium (K) 364 mg (8 %)
- Sodium, Na 180 mg (12%)

QUINOA PORRIDGE

Preparation time: 10 minutes

Cooking time: 0 minutes

Serving: 2

Ingredients:

1 cup cashew milk, warm

1 cup blueberries

2 cups quinoa, cooked

¼ cup chopped walnuts, toasted

2 teaspoons raw honey

½ teaspoon ground cinnamon

1 tablespoon chia seeds

Directions:

1. In a bowl, mix the cashew milk with the blueberries, quinoa, walnuts, honey, cinnamon, and chia seeds. Stir well, divide into 2 small bowls and serve.
2. Enjoy!

Nutrition:

- Calories 151
- Fat 2 g
- Fiber 11 g
- Carbs 14 g
- Protein 13 g

Preparation time: 5 minutes

Cooking time: 20 minutes

Serving: 4

Ingredients:

4 large apples, cut in rings

1 cup flour

¼ teaspoon baking powder

1 teaspoon stevia

¼ teaspoon cinnamon

1 large egg, beaten

1 cup milk

Vegetable oil, for frying

Cinnamon Topping:

⅓ cup of brown Swerve

2 teaspoons cinnamon

Directions:

1. Begin by mixing the flour with the baking powder, cinnamon, and stevia in a bowl.
2. Whisk the egg with the milk in a bowl.
3. Stir in the dry flour mixture and mix well until it makes a smooth batter.
4. Pour oil into a wok to deep fry the rings and heat it to 375 degrees F.
5. First, dip the apple in the flour batter and deep fry until golden brown.
6. Transfer the apple rings to a tray lined with a paper towel.
7. Drizzle the cinnamon and Swerve topping over the slices.
8. Serve fresh in the morning.

Nutrition:

- Calories 166,
- Total Fat 1.7g

- Saturated Fat 0.5g
- Cholesterol 33mg
- Sodium 55mg
- Carbohydrate 13.1g
- Dietary Fiber 1.9g
- Sugars 6.9g
- Protein 4.7g
- Calcium 65mg
- Phosphorous 241mg
- Potassium 197mg

CAULIFLOWER FRITTERS

Preparation Time: 10 minutes

Cooking Time: 15 minutes

Serving: 6 P

Ingredients:

1 large cauliflower head, cut into florets

2 eggs, beaten

½ teaspoon turmeric

½ teaspoon salt

¼ teaspoon black pepper

1 tablespoon coconut oil

Directions:

1. Place the cauliflower florets in a pot with water and bring to a boil. Cook until tender, around 5 minutes of boiling. Drain well.
2. Place the cauliflower, eggs, turmeric, salt, and pepper into the food processor.
3. Pulse until the mixture becomes coarse.
4. Transfer into a bowl. Using your hands, form six small flattened balls and place in the fridge for at least 1 hour until the mixture hardens.
5. Heat the oil in a nonstick pan and fry the cauliflower patties for 3 minutes on each side.

6. Serve and enjoy.

Nutrition:

- Calories 53,
- Total Fat 6g,
- Saturated Fat 2g,
- Total Carbs 2g,
- Net Carbs 1g,
- Protein 3g,
- Sugar: 1g,
- Fiber 1g,
- Sodium 228mg,
- Potassium 159mg

CAULIFLOWER HASH BROWN

Preparation Time: 10 minutes

Cooking Time: 20 minutes

Serving: 6

Ingredients:

4 eggs, beaten

½ cup coconut milk

½ teaspoon dry mustard

Salt and pepper to taste

1 large head cauliflower, shredded

Directions:

1. Place all ingredients in a mixing bowl and mix until well combined.
2. Place a nonstick frypan and heat over medium flame.
3. Add a large dollop of cauliflower mixture to the skillet.
4. Fry one side for 3 minutes, flip and cook the other side for a minute, like a pancake.
5. Repeat the process to the remaining ingredients.
6. Serve and enjoy.

Nutrition:

- Calories 102,

- Total Fat 8g,
- Saturated Fat 1g,
- Total Carbs 4g,
- Net Carbs 3g,
- Protein 5g,
- Sugar: 2g,
- Fiber 1g,
- Sodium 63mg,
- Potassium 251mg

ASPARAGUS FRITTATA

Preparation time: 5 minutes

Cooking time:30 minutes

Serving:4

Ingredients:

1/4 cup chopped parsley

1/2 tsp. onion powder

4 eggs

Pepper, to taste

2 tsp. EVOO, divided

10 medium trimmed asparagus spears

Directions:

1. Start by placing your oven at 450 F. Toss the asparagus spears with a teaspoon of oil and season with a bit of pepper.
2. Lay these out on a cookie sheet and bake for 20 minutes. Stir the spears occasionally and allow them to cook until they are tender and browned.
3. Beat the eggs together with the parsley and onion powder. Add pepper to taste.
4. Slice the asparagus into 1-inch pieces and lay them in the bottom of a medium pan.
5. Drizzle in the remaining oil and shake the pan so that everything distributes.

6. Pour the egg mixture over the asparagus and cook them over medium heat.

7. Once the eggs have set up on the bottom and almost set on the top, place a plate and flip over the pan so that the frittata is on the plate, and then carefully slide the frittata back in the pan to cook on the other side.

8. Allow this to continue cooking for 30 more seconds, or until set. Serve and enjoy!

Nutrition:

- Calories: 102
- Protein: 6 g
- Sodium: 46 mg
- Potassium: 248 mg
- Phosphorus: 103 mg

MEXICAN FRITTATA
_____

Preparation time: 5 minutes

Cooking time: 30 minutes

Serving: 4

Ingredients:

½ cup almond milk

5 large eggs

¼ cup onions, chopped

¼ cup green bell pepper, chopped

Directions:

1. Preheat the oven to 400° F.

2. Using a large bowl, combine almond milk, eggs, onion, and green bell pepper. Whisk until all ingredients are well combined.

3. Transfer the mixture to a baking dish. Bake for 20 minutes. Serve.

Nutrition:

- Protein 16.35g (30%)
- Potassium (K) 243 mg (5 %)
- Sodium, Na 216 mg (14%)

Preparation time: 10 minutes

Cooking time: 30 minutes

Serving: 4

Ingredients:

¼ cup coconut milk, unsweetened

6 eggs

1 yellow onion, chopped

4 ounces asparagus, chopped

2 tablespoons olive oil

2 cups baby spinach

A pinch of salt and black pepper

Directions:

1. Heat a pan with the oil over medium-high heat, add the onion, stir and cook for 2-3 minutes.
2. Add the asparagus, salt, and pepper, stir and cook for 2 minutes more.
3. In a bowl, mix the eggs with salt and pepper, stir well and pour over the asparagus.
4. Add the spinach, mix a bit, place in the oven, and bake at 360 degrees F for 25 minutes.
5. Slice the frittata and serve it for breakfast.
6. Enjoy!

Nutrition:

- Calories 200,
- Fat 3g,
- Fiber 6g,
- Carbs 14g,
- Protein 6g

Preparation time: 5 minutes

Cooking time: 30 minutes

Serving: 4

Ingredients:

1 tablespoon olive oil

1 cup yellow onion, sliced

3 cups zucchini, chopped

½ cup Swiss cheese, grated

8 large eggs

½ teaspoon black pepper

⅛ teaspoon paprika

3 tablespoons parsley, chopped

Directions:

1. Toss the zucchinis with the onion, parsley, and all other ingredients in a large bowl.
2. Pour this zucchini-garlic mixture into an 11x7 inches pan and spread it evenly.
3. Bake the zucchini casserole for approximately 35 minutes at 350 degrees F.
4. Cut in slices and serve.

Nutrition:

- Calories 142,
- Total Fat 9.7g
- Saturated Fat 2.8g
- Cholesterol 250mg
- Sodium 123mg
- Carbohydrate 4.7g
- Dietary Fiber 1.3g
- Sugars 2.4g
- Protein 10.2g
- Calcium 73mg

- Phosphorous 375mg
- Potassium 286mg

Tuna Salad

Preparation time: 5 minutes

Cooking time: 10 minutes

Serving: 4

Ingredients:

1 can of tuna, drained

1 cup onion, minced

1 celery, minced

Fresh herbs of choice

Directions:

1. In a salad bowl, put together tuna, mayonnaise, onion, celery, and fresh herbs of choice.
2. Mix all the ingredients until well combined. Serve.

Nutrition:

- Protein 21.89g (40%),
- Potassium (K) 284 mg (6 %)
- Sodium, Na 222 mg (15%)

Winter Fruit Salad

Preparation time: 10 minutes

Cooking time: 0 minutes

Serving: 6

Ingredients:

4 persimmons, cubed

4 pears, cubed

1 cup grapes, halved

1 cup apples, peeled, cored, and cubed

¾ cup basil nut, halved

1 tablespoon olive oil

1 tablespoon peanut oil

1 tablespoon pomegranate flavored vinegar

2 tablespoons agave nectar

Directions:

1. In a salad bowl, mix the persimmons with pears, grapes, apples, and basil nuts. In another bowl, mix the olive oil with the peanut oil, vinegar, and agave nectar. Whisk well then pour over the salad, toss and serve for breakfast.

2. Enjoy!

Nutrition:

- Calories 125,
- Fat 3g,
- Fiber 6g,
- Carbs 14g,
- Protein 8g

BUCKWHEAT GRANOLA

Preparation time: 10 minutes

Cooking time: 45 minutes

Serving: 6

Ingredients:

2 cups oats

1 cup buckwheat

1 cup apple puree

6 tablespoons coconut oil

5 tablespoons cocoa powder

1 teaspoon fresh grated ginger

Directions:

1. In a large bowl, mix the oats with the buckwheat, sunflower, apple puree, oil, cocoa powder, and ginger then stir well. Spread on a lined baking sheet, press well, and place in the oven at 360 degrees F for 45 minutes. Leave the granola to cool down, slice, and serve for breakfast.

2. Enjoy!

Nutrition:

- Calories 161,
- Fat 3g,
- Fiber 5g,
- Carbs 11g,
- Protein 7g

GARLIC MAYO BREAD

Preparation time: 5 minutes

Cooking time: 30 minutes

Serving: 4

Ingredients:

3 tablespoons vegetable oil

4 cloves garlic, minced

2 teaspoons paprika

Dash cayenne pepper

1 teaspoon lemon juice

2 tablespoons Swiss cheese, grated

3/4 cup mayonnaise

1 loaf (1 lb.) French bread, sliced

1 teaspoon Italian herbs

Directions:

1. Mix the garlic with the oil in a small bowl and leave it overnight.
2. Discard the garlic from the bowl and keep the garlic-infused oil.
3. Mix the garlic-oil with cayenne, paprika, lemon juice, mayonnaise, and Parmesan.
4. Place the bread slices in a baking tray lined with parchment paper.
5. Top these slices with the mayonnaise mixture and drizzle the Italian herbs on top.
6. Broil these slices for 5 minutes until golden brown.
7. Serve warm.

Nutrition:

- Calories 217,
- Total Fat 7.9g
- Saturated Fat 1.8g
- Cholesterol 5mg
- Sodium 423mg
- Carbohydrate 30.3g
- Dietary Fiber 1.3g
- Sugars 2g
- Protein 7g
- Calcium 56mg
- Phosphorous 347mg
- Potassium 72mg

PINEAPPLE BREAD

Preparation time: 5 minutes

Cooking time: 20 minutes

Serving: 4

Ingredients:

1/3 cup Swerve

1/3 cup butter, unsalted

2 eggs

2 cups flour

3 teaspoons baking powder

1 cup pineapple, undrained

6 mulberries, chopped

Directions:

1. Whisk the Swerve with the butter in a mixer until fluffy.
2. Stir in the eggs, then beat again.
3. Add the baking powder and flour, then mix well until smooth.
4. Fold in the cherries and pineapple.
5. Spread this mulberry-pineapple batter in a 9x5 inch baking pan.
6. Bake the pineapple batter for 1 hour at 350 degrees F.

7. Slice the bread and serve.

Nutrition:

- Calories 197,
- Total Fat 7.2g
- Saturated Fat 1.3g
- Cholesterol 33mg
- Sodium 85mg
- Carbohydrate 18.3g
- Dietary Fiber 1.1g
- Sugars 3 g
- Protein 4g
- Calcium 79mg
- Phosphorous 316mg
- Potassium 227mg

ZUCCHINI BREAD

Preparation time: 5 minutes

Cooking time: 40 minutes

Serving: 4

Ingredients:

3 eggs

1 1/2 cups Swerve

1 cup apple sauce

2 cups zucchini, shredded

1 teaspoon vanilla

2 cups flour

1/4 teaspoon baking powder

1 teaspoon baking soda

1 teaspoon cinnamon

1/2 teaspoon ginger

1 cup unsalted nuts, chopped

Directions:

1. Thoroughly whisk the eggs with the zucchini, apple sauce, and the rest of the ingredients in a bowl.
2. Once mixed evenly, spread the mixture in a loaf pan.
3. Bake it for 1 hour at 375 degrees F in a preheated oven.
4. Slice and serve.

Nutrition:

- Calories 200,
- Total Fat 5.4g
- Saturated Fat 0.9g
- Cholesterol 31mg
- Sodium 94mg
- Carbohydrate 26.9g
- Dietary Fiber 1.6g
- Sugars 16.3g
- Protein 4.4g
- Calcium 20mg
- Phosphorous 212mg
- Potassium 137mg

TEXAS TOAST CASSEROLE

Preparation time: 5 minutes

Cooking time:50 minutes

Serving:4

Ingredients:

1/2 cup butter, melted

1 cup brown Swerve

1 lb. Texas Toast bread, sliced

4 large eggs

1 1/2 cup milk

1 tablespoon vanilla extract

2 tablespoons Swerve

2 teaspoons cinnamon

Maple syrup for serving

Directions:

1. Layer a 9x13 inches baking pan with cooking spray.

2. Spread the bread slices at the bottom of the prepared pan.

3. Whisk the eggs with the remaining ingredients in a mixer.

4. Pour this mixture over the bread slices evenly.

5. Bake the bread for 30 minutes at 350 degrees F in a preheated oven.

6. Serve.

Nutrition:

- Calories 332,
- Total Fat 13.7g
- Saturated Fat 6.9g
- Cholesterol 102mg
- Sodium 350mg
- Carbohydrate 22.6g
- Dietary Fiber 2g
- Sugars 6g Protein 7.4g
- Calcium 143mg
- Phosphorous 186mg
- Potassium 74mg

AUBERGINE EGG BAKE

Preparation time: 5 minutes

Cooking time: 50 minutes

Serving: 4

Ingredients:

1 tbsp. chopped parsley

Pepper, to taste

4 eggs

2 large eggplants

2 tbsp canola oil,

Directions:

1. Start by placing the oven to 425 F.
2. Slice the eggplants in half lengthwise. Place them on a baking sheet, season with salt, and drizzle with canola oil. Roast the aubergines for 30 minutes.
3. Carefully crack one egg in a small bowl, making sure that the yolk doesn't break.
4. Using a spoon, take one scoop from the centre of the aubergine. Pour the egg into the center of one of the aubergine halves.
5. Repeat this for the other egg and the other aubergine half. Sprinkle with some pepper.
6. Bake for 15 minutes or until the eggs are set to your desired doneness.
7. Remove and sprinkle with the parsley before serving. Enjoy!

Nutrition:

- Calories: 242
- Protein: 9 g
- Sodium: 88 mg
- Potassium: 575 mg
- Phosphorus: 164 mg

OLIVE OIL AND SESAME ASPARAGUS

Preparation time: 5 minutes

Cooking time: 30 minutes

Serving: 4

Ingredients:

½ cup water

2 cups asparagus, sliced

½ tablespoon olive oil, add more for drizzling

1/8 teaspoon red pepper flakes, crushed

½ teaspoon sesame seeds

Directions:

1. In a large skillet, bring water to a boil.

2. Add in asparagus. Allow to boil for 2 minutes. Reduce the heat and cook for another 5 minutes. Drain asparagus and place on a plate. Set aside.

3. Meanwhile, heat the olive oil. Tip in asparagus and red pepper flakes. Saute for 3 minutes.

4. Remove from heat. Drizzle in more olive oil and sprinkle sesame seeds before serving.

Nutrition:

- Protein 6.19g (11%)
- Potassium (K) 547 mg (12 %)
- Sodium, Na 9 mg (1%)

ASPARAGUS AND CHEESE CREPES WITH PARSLEY

Preparation time: 5 minutes

Cooking time: 20 minutes

Serving: 4

Ingredients:

12 asparagus

4 oz. soft cheese

1/2 tsp. black pepper

1/3 cup flour

1/2 glass water

1/4 bowl cream

1 egg

2 egg whites

4 tbsp. butter

1-piece parsley

1 tsp. lemon juice

Directions:

1. Cook the asparagus for 6 to 8 minutes

2. Mix the softened cream cheese with parsley, spices, and lemon juice to prepare a sauce.

3. Put together the flour, water, egg, egg whites, and 2 tablespoons of butter already melted: mix everything to prepare a batter.

4. Prepare 8 to 10-inch crepe by melting the butter taken from 1/2 tablespoon, adding 1/3 of cup crepe batter, and turn the pan to spread the batter.

5. Cook it on both sides, cool it, and repeat to prepare 4 crepes.

6. Insert the cheese in the crepes that you are willing to roll afterward, putting inside also the asparagus.

7. Put them in the fridge for 1 hour. After that, cut the crepes rolls into 3 to 4 pieces. Serve and enjoy!

Nutrition:

- Calories: 305
- Protein: 10 g
- Sodium: 245 mg
- Potassium: 355 mg
- Phosphorus: 140 mg

Chapter 3

Lunch Recipes

ASIAN STYLE PAN-FRIED CHICKEN

Preparation time: 5 minutes

Cooking time: 20 minutes

Serving: 4

Ingredients:

1 lemon, cut into wedges

3 tsp. canola oil, divided

1/2 cup cornstarch

1 tsp. low sodium soy sauce

1-inch piece minced ginger

1 tsp. dry rice wine

1 cup Shiitake mushrooms

12 oz. chicken thighs, boneless and skinless

Directions:

1. Mix the soy sauce, ginger, rice wine, and chicken.
2. Toss everything together and allow it to marinate for 15 minutes.
3. Toss the chicken one more time and then drain off the liquid. One at a time, dip the chicken pieces into the cornstarch so that they are coated.
4. Heat 1.5 teaspoons of oil on medium-high in a medium skillet.
5. Sautè the shiitake mushrooms.
6. Add half of the chicken to the skillet and cook until it has turned golden brown on one side, around 3 to 5 minutes. Turn the chicken over and continue to cook until the chicken has cooked through and browned. Place on a plate lined with a paper towel to cool and to absorb excess oil.
7. Add in the remaining oil and cook the rest of the chicken thighs.
8. Serve the chicken with a garnish of lemon. Enjoy!

Nutrition:

- Calories: 198
- Protein: 17 g
- Sodium: 119 mg
- Potassium: 218 mg
- Phosphorus: 148 mg

CURRIED CHICKEN WITH CAULIFLOWER

Preparation time: 5 minutes

Cooking time: 30 minutes

Serving: 4

Ingredients:

Lime juice of 2 limes

1/2 tsp. dried oregano

Cauliflower head, cut into florets

4 tsp. EVOO, divided

6 chicken thighs, bone-in

1/2 tsp. pepper, divided

1/4 tsp. paprika

1/2 tsp. ground cumin

3 tbsp. curry powder

Directions:

1. Mix a quarter of a tsp. of pepper, paprika, cumin, and curry in a small bowl.
2. Add the chicken thighs to a medium bowl and drizzle with 2 tsp. olive oil and sprinkle in the curry mixture.
3. Toss them together so that the chicken is well coated.
4. Cover this up and refrigerate it for at least 2 hours.
5. Now set your oven to 400 F.
6. Toss the cauliflower, remaining oil, and oregano together in a medium bowl. Arrange the cauliflower and chicken across a baking sheet in one layer.
7. Allow this to bake for 40 minutes. Stir the cauliflower and flip the chicken once during the cooking time. The chicken should be browned and the juices should run clear. The temperature of the chicken should reach 165.
8. Serve with some lime juice. Enjoy!

Nutrition:

- Calories: 175
- Protein: 16 g
- Sodium: 77 mg
- Potassium: 486 mg
- Phosphorus: 152 mg

OREGANO SEABASS WITH CRUNCHY CRUST

Preparation Time: 10 minutes

Cooking time: 2 hours

Serving:2

Ingredients:

8 oz seabass fillet

2 tablespoons panko breadcrumbs

1 oz Parmesan, grated

1 teaspoon dried oregano

1 teaspoon sunflower oil

Directions:

1. In the mixing bowl combine panko bread crumbs, Parmesan, and dried oregano.

2. Sprinkle the fish with olive oil and coat in the breadcrumbs mixture.

3. After this, line the baking tray with baking paper.

4. Place the seabags in the tray and transfer in the preheated to the 385F oven.

5. Bake the fish for 25 minutes.

Nutrition:

*   Calories 245,
*   Fat 12.8g,
*   Fiber 0.6g,
*   Carbs 5.9g,
*   Protein 27.5g

SEABASS FISH CAKES

Preparation Time: 10 minutes

Cooking time: 10 minutes

Serving:4

Ingredients:

11 oz sea bass

1/3 cup shallot, chopped

1 teaspoon chili flakes

½ teaspoon salt

2 tablespoon wheat flour, whole grain

1 egg, beaten

1 tablespoon chives, chopped

1 teaspoon olive oil

1 teaspoon butter

Directions:

1. Put the butter in the skillet and melt it.
2. Add shallot and cook it until translucent.
3. After this, transfer the shallot to the mixing bowl.
4. Add sea bass, chili flakes, salt, flour, egg, chives, and mix up until smooth with the help of the fork.
5. Make the medium size cakes and place them in the skillet.
6. Add olive oil.
7. Roast the fish cakes for 3 minutes from each side over medium heat.
8. Dry the cooked fish cakes with a paper towel if needed and transfer them to the serving plates.

Nutrition:

- Calories 221,
- Fat 12.2g,
- Fiber 0.1g,
- Carbs 5.4g,
- Protein 21.3g

CAJUN CATFISH

Preparation Time: 10 minutes

Cooking time: 10 minutes

Serving:4

Ingredients:

16 oz catfish steaks (4 oz each fish steak)

1 tablespoon cajun spices

1 egg, beaten

1 tablespoon sunflower oil

Directions:

1. Pour sunflower oil into the skillet and preheat it until shimmering.
2. Meanwhile, dip every catfish steak in the beaten egg and coat it in Cajun spices.

3. Place the fish steaks in the hot oil and roast them for 4 minutes from each side.
4. The cooked catfish steaks should have a light brown crust.

Nutrition:
- Calories 263,
- Fat 16.7g,
- Fiber 0g,
- Carbs 0.1g,
- Protein 26.3g

TERIYAKI TUNA

Preparation Time: 10 minutes

Cooking time: 6 minutes

Serving:3

Ingredients:

3 tuna fillets

3 teaspoons low sodium teriyaki sauce

½ teaspoon minced garlic

1 teaspoon olive oil

Directions:
1. Whisk together teriyaki sauce, minced garlic, and olive oil.
2. Brush every tuna fillet with teriyaki mixture.
3. Preheat grill to 390F.
4. Grill the fish for 3 minutes from each side.

Nutrition:
- Calories 382,
- Fat 32.6,
- Fiber 0,
- Carbs 1.1,
- Protein 21.4

Preparation Time: 10 minutes

Cooking time: 10 minutes

Serving:3

Ingredients:

14 oz. trout fillets

1/2 teaspoon herb seasoning blend

1 lemon, sliced

2 green onions, sliced

1 stalk celery, chopped

1 medium carrot, julienne

Directions:

1. Prepare and preheat a charcoal grill over moderate heat.
2. Place the trout fillets over a large piece of foil and drizzle herb seasoning on top.
3. Spread the lemon slices, carrots, celery, and green onions over the fish.
4. Cover the fish with foil and pack it.
5. Place the packed fish in the grill and cook for 15 minutes.
6. Once done, remove the foil from the fish.
7. Serve.

Nutrition:

- Calories 202
- Total Fat 8.5g
- Saturated Fat 1.5g
- Cholesterol 73mg
- Sodium 82mg
- Carbohydrate 3.5g
- Dietary Fiber 1.1g
- Sugars 1.3g
- Protein 26.9g
- Calcium 70mg

- Phosphorous 287mg
- Potassium 560mg

CITRUS GLAZED SOLE

Preparation Time: 10 minutes

Cooking time: 20 minutes

Serving:3

Ingredients:

2 garlic cloves, crushed

1 1/2 tablespoons lemon juice

2 tablespoons olive oil

1 tablespoon butter

1 tablespoon Dijon mustard

2 dashes cayenne pepper

1 teaspoon dried basil leaves

1 teaspoon dried dill

24 oz. sole filet

Directions:

1. Place a 1-quart saucepan over moderate heat and add the oil, butter, garlic, lemon juice, mustard, cayenne pepper, dill, and basil to the pan.
2. Stir this mixture for 5 minutes after it has boiled.
3. Prepare and preheat a charcoal grill over moderate heat.
4. Place the fish on a foil sheet and fold the edges to make a foil tray.
5. Pour the prepared sauce over the fish.
6. Place the fish in the foil in the preheated grill and cook for 12 minutes.
7. Slice and serve.

Nutrition:

- Calories 401
- Total Fat 20.5g
- Saturated Fat 5.3g

- Cholesterol 144mg
- Sodium 256mg
- Carbohydrate 0.5g
- Dietary Fiber 0.2g
- Sugars 0.1g
- Protein 48.4g
- Calcium 549mg
- Phosphorous 214mg
- Potassium 446mg

BROILED COD FILLETS

Preparation Time: 10 minutes

Cooking time: 30 minutes

Serving: 3

Ingredients:

1 tablespoon ginger root, grated

1 clove garlic, minced

¼ cup maple syrup

1 tablespoon hot pepper sauce

4 cod fillets, skinless

Directions:

1. Grease a pan with cooking spray and place it over moderate heat.
2. Add the ginger and garlic and sauté for 3 minutes then transfer to a bowl.
3. Add the hot pepper sauce and maple syrup to the ginger-garlic.
4. Mix well and keep this mixture aside.
5. Place the cod fillet in a suitable baking tray, greased with cooking oil.
6. Brush the maple sauce over the fillets liberally
7. Broil them for 10 minutes in the oven at broiler settings.
8. Serve warm.

Nutrition:

- Calories 289

- Total Fat 11.1g
- Saturated Fat 1.6g
- Cholesterol 78mg
- Sodium 80mg
- Carbohydrate 13.6g
- Dietary Fiber 0g
- Sugars 11.8g
- Protein 34.6g
- Calcium 78mg
- Phosphorous 230mg
- Potassium 331mg

RED GRAPES CHICKEN SALAD WITH CURRY

Preparation Time: 10 minutes

Cooking time: 30 minutes

Serving: 3

Ingredients:

1 apple

1/2 bowl seedless, red grapes

4 cooked skinless and boneless chicken breasts

1-piece celery

1/2 bowl onion

1/2 bowl canned water chestnuts

1/2 tsp. curry powder

3/4 cup mayonnaise

1/8 tsp. black pepper

Directions:

1. Cut the chicken into small dices and chop celery, onion, and apple. Drain and cut chestnuts.
2. Put together the chicken pieces, celery, onion, apple, grapes, water chestnuts, pepper, curry powder, and mayonnaise.
3. Serve it in a big salad bowl. Enjoy!

Nutrition:

- Calories: 235
- Protein: 13 g
- Sodium: 160 mg
- Potassium: 200 mg
- Phosphorus: 115 mg

LEMONY HADDOCK

Preparation time: 10 minutes

Cooking Time:20 minutes

Serving: 4

Ingredients:

1 tablespoon melted unsalted butter

12ounces haddock fillets, deboned and skinned

½ cup bread crumbs

3 tablespoons chopped fresh parsley

1 tablespoon lemon zest

1 teaspoon chopped fresh thyme

¼ teaspoon black pepper (ground)

Directions:

1. Preheat an oven to 350^0F.
2. In a mixing bowl, add bread crumbs, parsley, lemon zest, thyme, and pepper. Combine to mix well with each other.
3. Add butter and combine until you get crumbles.
4. Take a baking sheet and place the haddock over. Add crumb mixture on top.
5. Bake for 18-20 minutes until evenly brown from the top.
6. Serve warm.

Nutrition:

- Calories: 183
- Fat: 4g
- Phosphorus: 233mg
- Potassium: 305mg

- Sodium: 316mg
- Carbohydrates: 9g
- Protein: 16g

GLAZED SEABASS

Preparation time: 10 minutes

Cooking Time: 10 minutes

Serving: 4

Ingredients:

4 (3-ounce) seabags fillets

1 tablespoon olive oil

2 tablespoons honey

1 teaspoon lemon zest

½ teaspoon Black pepper (ground), to taste

½ scallion, chopped

Directions:

1. Pat dry the fish with paper towels.
2. In a mixing bowl, add honey, lemon zest, and pepper. Combine to mix well with each other.
3. Add your cod and coat evenly.
4. Take a medium saucepan or skillet, add oil. Heat over medium heat.
5. Add the cod and stir-cook until light brown and cooked well, about 8-10 minutes. Flip in between.
6. Serve warm with scallions on top.

Nutrition:

- Calories: 238
- Fat: 13g
- Phosphorus: 220mg
- Potassium: 348mg
- Sodium: 74mg
- Carbohydrates: 10g
- Protein: 16g

Preparation time: 10 minutes

Cooking Time:5 minutes

Serving: 4

Ingredients:

2 teaspoons garlic, minced

Pinch sea salt

2 tablespoons olive oil

2 tablespoons lemon juice

1 tablespoon chopped fresh parsley

1 tablespoon chopped fresh oregano

Pinch black pepper (ground)

½ pound cleaned calamari

Lemon wedges

Directions:

1. In a mixing bowl, add olive oil, lemon juice, parsley, oregano, garlic, salt, and pepper. Combine to mix well with each other.

2. Add calamari and combine again. Refrigerate to marinate for 1 hour.

3. Preheat grill over medium heat setting, grease grates with some oil.

4. Grill calamari for 3 minutes totals until evenly cooked. Turn halfway through.

5. Serve warm with some lemon wedges.

Nutrition:

- Calories: 103
- Fat: 6g
- Phosphorus: 130mg
- Potassium: 176mg
- Sodium: 73mg
- Carbohydrates: 2g
- Protein: 4g

Preparation time: 10 minutes

Cooking Time: 30 minutes

Serving: 6

Ingredients:

4 tablespoons green pepper, chopped

2 tablespoons green onions, chopped

1 cup celery, chopped

1 cup crabmeat, cooked (boiled)

1 cup shrimp, cooked (boiled)

½ cup frozen green peas, thawed

½ teaspoon black pepper

½ cup mayonnaise

1 cup bread crumbs

Directions:

1. Preheat an oven to 375°F. Grease a casserole dish with some cooking spray.
2. In a mixing bowl, add all ingredients except bread crumbs. Combine to mix well with each other.
3. Add the mixture to a casserole dish and bake for 30 minutes until evenly brown.
4. Serve warm.

Nutrition:

- Calories: 268
- Fat: 7g
- Phosphorus: 159mg
- Potassium: 287mg
- Sodium: 466mg
- Carbohydrates: 21g
- Protein: 17g

Preparation time: 10 minutes

Cooking Time: 15 minutes

Serving: 4

Ingredients:

2 teaspoons minced garlic

4 ounces shrimp, peeled, deveined, and chopped

1 tablespoon chopped fresh basil

½ cup heavy (whipping) cream

Black pepper (ground), to taste

½ cup dry white wine

4 ounces uncooked linguine

1 teaspoon olive oil

Juice of 1 lemon

Directions:

1. Cook pasta as directed overpack; drain and set aside.
2. Take a medium saucepan or skillet, add oil. Heat over medium heat.
3. Add shrimps and garlic, stir-cook until become opaque for 5-6 minutes.
4. Add wine, lemon juice, and basil; stir-cook for 5 minutes.
5. Add cream, combine, and simmer for 2 minutes.
6. Add pasta and coat well.
7. Serve warm.

Nutrition:

- Calories: 238
- Fat: 7g
- Phosphorus: 143mg
- Potassium: 167mg
- Sodium: 68mg
- Carbohydrates: 22g
- Protein: 12g

Preparation time: 10 minutes

Cooking Time: 15 minutes

Serving: 4

Ingredients:

1¾ pound lean ground chicken

2 tablespoons sesame oil

1 medium onion, chopped

1 cup celery, chopped

6 garlic cloves, minced

2 cups asparagus, trimmed and cut into 1-inch pieces

1/3 cup coconut aminos

2½ teaspoons ginger powder

2 tablespoons organic coconut crystals

1 tablespoon arrowroot starch

1 tablespoon cold water

¼ teaspoon red pepper flakes, crushed

Directions:

1. Heat a substantial nonstick skillet on medium-high heat.
2. Add chicken and cook for approximately 5-7 minutes or till browned.
3. With a slotted spoon transfer the chicken inside a bowl and discard the grease from the skillet.
4. In the same skillet, heat oil on medium heat.
5. Add onion, celery, and garlic and sauté for about 5 minutes.
6. Add asparagus and cooked chicken minimizing the temperature to medium-low.
7. Meanwhile inside a pan mix coconut aminos, ginger powder, and coconut crystals n medium heat and convey to some boil.
8. In a smaller bowl, mix arrowroot starch and water.
9. Slowly, add arrowroot mixture, stirring continuously.
10. Cook for approximately 2-3 minutes.

11. Add the sauce in the skillet with chicken mixture and stir to blend.
12. Stir in red pepper flakes and cook for approximately 2-3 minutes.
13. Serve hot.

Nutrition:

- Calories: 309,
- Fat: 20g,
- Carbohydrates: 19g,
- Fiber: 2g,
- Protein: 28g

GROUND CHICKEN WITH PEAS & CARROTS

Preparation time: 10 minutes

Cooking Time: 25 minutes

Serving: 4

Ingredients:

3-4 tablespoons coconut oil

1-pound lean ground chicken

1-2 fresh red chiles, chopped

1 onion, chopped

Salt, to taste

2 minced garlic cloves

1 (1-inch) piece fresh ginger, grated finely

1 tablespoon curry powder

1 teaspoon ground coriander

1 teaspoon ground cumin

1 teaspoon ground turmeric

7 carrots, peeled and cut into 1-inch size

½ cup water

1 cup fresh peas, shelled

2 plum tomatoes, chopped

1 cup shiitake mushrooms

½ cup fresh cilantro, chopped

Directions:

1. In a substantial pan, heat oil on medium-high heat.
2. Add chicken and cook for about 4-5 minutes.
3. Add chiles and onion and cook for about 4-5 minutes.
4. Add garlic and ginger and cook for approximately 1-2 minutes.
5. Stir in spices, shiitake mushrooms, carrots, and water and convey to your boil.
6. Reduce the warmth to medium-low.
7. Simmer covered approximately 15-twenty or so minutes.
8. Add peas and tomatoes and cook for about 2-3 minutes.
9. Serve using the garnishing of cilantro.

Nutrition:

- Calories: 452,
- Fat: 14g,
- Carbohydrates: 24g,
- Fiber: 13g,
- Protein: 36g

CHICKEN & TURNIPS CHILI

Preparation Time: 15 minutes

Cooking Time: 41 minutes

Serving: 4-6

Ingredients:

2 tablespoons extra-virgin olive oil

1 green bell pepper, seeded and chopped

1 small yellow onion, chopped

2 garlic cloves, chopped finely

1-pound lean ground chicken

1 (15-ounce) turnips puree

14 ½-ounce diced tomatoes with liquid

1 teaspoon ground cumin

½ teaspoon ground turmeric

½ teaspoon ground cinnamon

1 cup water

1 (15-ounce) can chickpeas, rinsed and drained

Directions:

1. In a big pan, heat oil on medium-low heat.

2. Add the bell pepper, onion, and garlic and sauté for approximately 5 minutes.

3. Add chicken and cook for about 5-6 minutes.

4. Add tomatoes, turnip puree, spices, and water and convey to your boil on high heat.

5. Reduce the temperature to medium-low heat and stir in chickpeas.

6. Simmer, covered for approximately a half-hour, stirring occasionally.

7. Serve hot.

Nutrition:

- Calories: 437,
- Fat: 17g,
- Carbohydrates: 29g,
- Fiber: 16g,
- Protein: 42g

CHICKEN & VEGGIES CHILI

Preparation Time: 15 minutes

Cooking Time: 35 minutes

Serving: 8

Ingredients:

3 tablespoons essential olive oil, divided

1½ pound lean ground chicken

2 tablespoons tomato paste

1 teaspoon dried oregano, crushed

1 teaspoon ground coriander

1 teaspoon ground cumin

½ teaspoon ground cinnamon

½ teaspoon ground turmeric

1½ cups chicken broth

3 cups cooked sprouted beans trio

½ cup mild salsa

2 carrots, peeled and chopped

1 (14½-ounce) can crushed tomatoes

1 medium onion, chopped

2 garlic cloves, chopped finely

3 medium zucchinis, chopped

1 cup Swiss cheese

4 scallions, chopped

Directions:

1. In a sizable pan, heat 1 tablespoon of oil on medium-high heat.
2. Add chicken and with the spoon, plunge into pieces.
3. Add tomato paste, oregano, and spices and cook for about 4-5 minutes.
4. Add broth and provide to a boil,
5. Reduce the temperature to medium and simmer for around 5 minutes.
6. Add beans trio, salsa, carrots, and tomatoes, and simmer for about 10 minutes.
7. Meanwhile, in a substantial skillet, heat the remaining oil on medium-high heat.
8. Add onion and garlic and sauté for about 5 minutes.
9. Add zucchini and cook for approximately 5 minutes, stirring occasionally.
10. Transfer the zucchini mixture within the chili mixture and transfer the warmth to low.
11. Simmer for around 15 minutes.

Nutrition:

- Calories: 411,
- Fat: 10g,
- Carbohydrates: 19g,

- Fiber: 14g,
- Protein: 37g

Preparation Time: 15 minutes

Cooking Time: 30 minutes

Serving: 8

Ingredients:

2 cups rice vermicelli

4 oz cooked sea bass

2 oz frozen prawns, thawed

4 tablespoons vegetable oil

1 onion, shredded

2 cups bean sprouts

1 teaspoon salt

1 tablespoon curry powder

2 tablespoons low-sodium soy sauce

2 green or red chili peppers

2 spring onions, shredded

Directions:

1. Soak rice vermicelli in boiling water for 10 minutes. Rinse in cold water.
2. Slice pork meat thinly. Dry prawns in a paper towel.
3. Heat oil in a wok. Stir fry onion and beans for 2 minutes.
4. Add noodles, sea bass, and prawns. Stir for 3 minutes.
5. Tip in curry powder, soy sauce, chili peppers, and spring onions. Stir fry for 1 minute. Serve.

Nutrition:

- Protein 24.81g (46%),
- Potassium (K) 650 mg (14%) and
- Sodium, Na 215 mg (14%)

Preparation Time: 15 minutes

Cooking Time: 30 minutes

Serving: 8

Ingredients:

2 cups rice vermicelli

4 oz cooked beef

2 oz frozen prawns, thawed

4 tablespoons vegetable oil

1 onion, shredded

2 cups bean sprouts

1 teaspoon salt

1 tablespoon curry powder

2 tablespoons low-sodium soy sauce

2 green or red chili peppers

2 spring onions, shredded

Directions:

1. Soak rice vermicelli in boiling water for 10 minutes. Rinse in cold water.
2. Slice beef meat thinly. Dry prawns in a paper towel.
3. Heat oil in a wok. Stir fry onion and beans for 2 minutes.
4. Add noodles, beef, and prawns. Stir for 3 minutes.
5. Tip in curry powder, soy sauce, chili peppers, and spring onions. Stir fry for 1 minute. Serve.

Nutrition:

- Protein 14.3g (26%),
- Potassium (K) 460 mg (10%) and
- Sodium, Na 888 mg (59%),
- Content of Sodium without added salt 307mg (20%)

Preparation Time: 15 minutes

Cooking Time: 35 minutes

Serving: 8

Ingredients:

2 cups rice vermicelli

4 oz cooked chicken

2 oz frozen prawns, thawed

4 tablespoons vegetable oil

1 onion, shredded

2 cups bean sprouts

1 teaspoon salt

1 tablespoon curry powder

2 tablespoons low-sodium soy sauce

2 green or red chili peppers

2 spring onions, shredded

Directions:

1. Soak rice vermicelli in boiling water for 10 minutes. Rinse in cold water.
2. Slice chicken meat thinly. Dry prawns in a paper towel.
3. Heat oil in a wok. Stir fry onion and beans for 2 minutes.
4. Add noodles, chicken, and prawns. Stir for 3 minutes.
5. Tip in curry powder, soy sauce, chili peppers, and spring onions. Stir fry for 1 minute. Serve.

Nutrition:

- Protein 14.31g (26%),
- Potassium (K) 431 mg (9%) and
- Sodium, Na 885 mg (59%),
- Without added salt content of Sodium is 304mg (20%)

Preparation time:5 minutes

Cooking time:20 minutes

Serving:4

Ingredients:

1 whole river trout

1 tsp. thyme

¼ diced yellow pepper

1 cup baby spinach leaves

¼ diced green pepper

1 juiced lime

¼ diced red pepper

1 tsp. oregano

1 tsp. extra virgin olive oil

1 tsp. black pepper

Directions:

1. Preheat the broiler /grill on high heat.
2. Lightly oil a baking tray.
3. Mix all of the ingredients apart from the trout and lime.
4. Slice the trout lengthways (there should be an opening here from where it was gutted) and stuff the mixed ingredients inside.
5. Squeeze the lime juice over the fish and then place the lime wedges on the tray.
6. Place under the broiler on the baking tray and broil for 15-20 minutes or until fish is thoroughly cooked through and flakes easily.
7. Enjoy alone or with a side helping of rice or salad.

Nutrition:

- Calories 290,
- Protein 15 g,
- Carbs 0 g,
- Fat 7 g,

- Sodium (Na) 43 mg,
- Potassium (K) 315 mg,
- Phosphorus 189 mg

HADDOCK & BUTTERED LEEKS

Preparation time: 5 minutes

Cooking time: 15 minutes

Serving: 2

Ingredients:

1 tbsp. unsalted butter

1 sliced leek

¼ tsp. black pepper

2 tsps. Chopped parsley

6 oz. haddock fillets

½ juiced lemon

Directions:

1. Preheat the oven to 375°F/Gas Mark 5.
2. Add the haddock fillets to baking or parchment paper and sprinkle with the black pepper.
3. Squeeze over the lemon juice and wrap into a parcel.
4. Bake the parcel on a baking tray for 10-15 minutes or until the fish is thoroughly cooked through.
5. Meanwhile, heat the butter over medium-low heat in a small pan.
6. Add the leeks and parsley and sauté for 5-7 minutes until soft.
7. Serve the haddock fillets on a bed of buttered leeks and enjoy!

Nutrition:

- Calories 124,
- Protein 15 g,
- Carbs 0 g,
- Fat 7 g,
- Sodium (Na) 161 mg,
- Potassium (K) 251 mg,
- Phosphorus 220 mg

Preparation time:5 minutes

Cooking time:20 minutes

Serving:2

Ingredients:

2 tbsps. coconut oil

1 cup white rice

¼ tsp. black pepper

½ diced red chili

1 tbsp. fresh basil

2 pressed garlic cloves

4 oz. halibut fillet

1 halved lime

2 sliced green onions

1 lime leaf

Directions:

1. Preheat oven to 400°F/Gas Mark 5.

2. Add half of the ingredients into baking paper and fold into a parcel.

3. Repeat for your second parcel.

4. Add to the oven for 15-20 minutes or until fish is thoroughly cooked through.

5. Serve with cooked rice.

Nutrition:

- Calories 311,
- Protein 16 g,
- Carbs 17 g,
- Fat 15 g,
- Sodium (Na) 31 mg,
- Potassium (K) 418 mg,
- Phosphorus 257 mg

Preparation time:5 minutes

Cooking time:10 minutes

Serving:2

Ingredients:

1 egg

½ cup green beans

¼ sliced cucumber

1 juiced lemon

1 tsp. black pepper

¼ sliced red onion

1 tbsp. olive oil

1 tbsp. capers

4 oz. cooked sea bags

4 iceberg lettuce leaves

1 tsp. chopped fresh cilantro

Directions:

1. Prepare the salad by washing and slicing the lettuce, cucumber, and onion.
2. Add to a salad bowl.
3. Mix 1 tbsp oil with the lemon juice, cilantro, and capers for a salad dressing. Set aside.
4. Boil a pan of water on high heat then lower to simmer and add the egg for 6 minutes. (Steam the green beans over the same pan in a steamer/colander for 6 minutes).
5. Remove the egg and rinse under cold water.
6. Peel before slicing in half.
7. Mix the pre cooked sea bass, salad, and dressing together in a salad bowl.
8. Toss to coat.
9. Top with the egg and serve with a sprinkle of black pepper.

Nutrition:

- Calories 199,
- Protein 19 g,
- Carbs 7 g,
- Fat 8 g,
- Sodium (Na) 466 mg,
- Potassium (K) 251 mg,
- Phosphorus 211 mg

MONK-FISH CURRY

Preparation time:5 minutes

Cooking time:20 minutes

Serving:2

Ingredients:

1 garlic clove

3 finely chopped green onions

1 tsp. grated ginger

1 cup water.

2 tsps. Chopped fresh basil

1 cup cooked rice noodles

1 tbsp. coconut oil

½ sliced red chili

4 oz. Monk-fish fillet

½ finely sliced stick lemongrass

2 tbsps. chopped shallots

Directions:

1. Slice the Monk-fish into bite-size pieces.
2. Using a pestle and mortar or food processor, crush the basil, garlic, ginger, chili, and lemon-grass to form a paste.
3. Heat the oil in a large wok or pan over medium-high heat and add the shallots.
4. Now add the water to the pan and bring to a boil.

5. Add the Monk-fish, lower the heat and cover to simmer for 10 minutes or until cooked through.

6. Enjoy with rice noodles and scatter with green onions to serve.

Nutrition:

- Calories 249,
- Protein 12 g,
- Carbs 30 g,
- Fat 10 g,
- Sodium (Na) 32 mg,
- Potassium (K) 398 mg,
- Phosphorus 190 mg

CANTONESE STYLE PORK ROAST

Preparation time:5 minutes

Cooking time:20 minutes

Serving:2

Ingredients:

2 cups cooked rice

For the Basting liquid

2 drops sesame oil

2 tablespoons honey

1 tablespoon char siu sauce

For the Pork and Marinade

2 pounds of pork shoulder

2 garlic cloves, thinly sliced

1 piece ginger, thinly sliced

2 tablespoons low-sodium soy sauce

2 tablespoons water

1 tablespoon char siu sauce

1 tablespoon honey

1 tablespoon oyster sauce

1 tablespoon rice wine

½ tablespoon fermented red bean curd

½ teaspoon five-spice powder

Directions:

1. Place pork and marinade ingredients in a food-safe bag; seal. Massage contents of the bag to mix; chill in the fridge for at least an hour (or up to 48 hours beforehand.) Discard garlic and ginger before roasting; reserve marinade.

2. Combine basting liquid ingredients in a small bowl.

3. Preheat oven to 400°F/200°C for at least 10 minutes. Place pork on the grill, preferably on a layered, deep baking sheet lined with aluminum foil. Pour leftover marinade into a baking dish. Place on the middle rack of the oven, and roast for 30 minutes. Using a pastry brush, baste meat in 10-minute intervals with prepared liquid.

4. After 30 minutes, remove pork from the oven. Set on a countertop to cool slightly before serving. If there is leftover basting liquid and marinade, brush liberally on meat. When pork is cool enough to handle, slice thinly; spoon equal portions into plates with rice.

Nutrition:

- Protein 28.2g (52%),
- Potassium (K) 560 mg (12%) and
- Sodium, Na 395 mg (26%)

CRISPY AND SPICY PORK

Preparation time:5 minutes

Cooking time:30 minutes

Serving:2

Ingredients:

1 pound boneless pork roast

1 garlic clove, minced

½ tablespoon honey

½ tablespoon coriander seeds

¼ teaspoon anise seed

¼ teaspoon cardamom

1/8 teaspoon black pepper

1/8 teaspoon allspice

¼ teaspoon cardamom

1/16 teaspoon crumbled dried mint

Directions:

1. Score the roast using inch sized cubes.
2. Crush the coriander seeds in a plastic bag using a rolling pin. Transfer to a bowl.
3. Add the rest of the ingredients to the coriander seeds and mix well. Rub the mixture all over the pork. Cover and marinate in the refrigerator for 1 hour.
4. Set the oven to 350°F.
5. Bake for 1 hour, or until the internal temperature of the pork is 160°F.

Nutrition:

- Protein 42.85g (78%),
- Potassium (K) 877 mg (19%) and
- Sodium, Na 150 mg (10%)

GARLIC PORK CHOPS IN TERIYAKI SAUCE

Preparation time:5 minutes

Cooking time:30 minutes

Serving:2

Ingredients:

3 pork chops

4 tablespoons low-sodium teriyaki sauce

1 teaspoon garlic powder

Directions:

1. Pour the teriyaki sauce over the pork chops, then season with garlic powder on both sides.
2. Grill the pork chops for 5 minutes per side, basting with the teriyaki sauce frequently.

Nutrition:

- Protein 42.02g (77%),
- Potassium (K) 607 mg (13%) and
- Sodium, Na 514 mg (34%)

CITRUS PORK CHOPS

Preparation time:5 minutes

Cooking time:20 minutes

Serving:2

Ingredients:

1 tsp canola oil

2 boneless pork chops, ½ inch thick each

¼ cup chopped leek, white and light green parts only

1 small garlic clove, minced

½ tablespoon cornstarch

2 ½ tablespoons freshly squeezed lime juice

1 tablespoon water

½ teaspoon honey

¼ teaspoon freshly grated orange zest

¼ teaspoon ground ginger

Pinch of sea salt

Pinch of ground black pepper

Directions:

1. Season the pork with salt and pepper. Coat with cornstarch.
2. Place a frying pan over medium flame and heat through. Once hot, add the oil and swirl to coat.
3. Cook the pork chops for 4 minutes per side, or until cooked through. Transfer to a platter and set aside.
4. Stir the garlic and leek in the same pan. Sauté until tender. Add the rest of the ingredients. Mix well. Simmer for 2 minutes or until thickened.
5. Return the pork chops into the pan. Simmer until heated through.

Nutrition:

- Protein 42.34g (78%),
- Potassium (K) 863 mg (18%) and
- Sodium, Na 173 mg (12%)

GROUND TURKEY WITH CHICKPEAS

Preparation Time: 15 minutes

Cooking Time: 35 minutes

Serving: 8

Ingredients:

3 tablespoons olive oil, divided

1 onion, chopped

1 tablespoon fresh ginger, minced

4 garlic cloves, minced

3 celery stalks, chopped

1 large carrot, peeled and chopped

1 cup dried chickpeas, rinsed, soaked for thirty minutes, and drained

2 cups chicken broth

1 teaspoon black mustard seeds

1½ teaspoons cumin seeds

1 teaspoon ground turmeric

½ teaspoon paprika

1-pound lean ground turkey

1 Serrano chile, seeded and chopped

2 scallions, chopped

Chopped fresh cilantro, for garnishing

Directions:

1. In a Dutch oven, heat 1 tablespoon of oil on medium heat.
2. Add onion, ginger, and garlic and sauté for around 5 minutes.
3. Stir in celery, carrot, chickpeas, and broth and convey to your boil
4. Reduce the warmth to medium-low.
5. Simmer, covered for around thirty minutes.
6. Meanwhile, in a skillet, heat the remaining oil on medium heat.

7. Add mustard seeds and cumin seeds and sauté for approximately 30 seconds.
8. Add turmeric and paprika and sauté for approximately 25 seconds.
9. Transfer a combination into a small bowl and aside.
10. In the same skillet, add turkey and cook for around 4-5 minutes.
11. Add Serrano chile and scallion and cook for about 3-4 minutes.
12. Add spiced oil mixture and stir to mix well.
13. Transfer the turkey mixture to simmering chickpeas and simmer for around 5-10 minutes more.

Nutrition:
- Calories: 422,
- Fat: 9g,
- Carbohydrates: 17g,
- Fiber: 14g,
- Protein: 37g

ROASTED WHOLE TURKEY

Preparation Time: 15 minutes

Cooking Time: 3 hours 30 minutes

Serving: 8-10

Ingredients:

For Turkey Marinade:

1 (2-inch) piece fresh ginger, grated finely

3 large garlic cloves, crushed

1 green chili, chopped finely

1 teaspoon fresh lemon zest, grated finely

5-ounce soy yogurt

3 tablespoons tomato puree

2 tablespoons fresh lemon juice

1 tablespoon ground cumin

1½ tablespoons garam masala

2 teaspoons ground turmeric

For Turkey:

1 (9-pound) whole turkey, giblets, and neck removed

Salt and freshly ground black pepper, to taste

1 garlic clove, halved

1 lime, halved

½ of lemon

Directions:

1. In a bowl, mix all marinade ingredients.
2. With a fork, pierce the turkey completely.
3. In a sizable baking dish, put the turkey.
4. Rub the turkey with marinade mixture evenly.
5. Refrigerate to marinate overnight.
6. Remove from refrigerator and make aside approximately a half-hour before serving.
7. Preheat the oven to 390 degrees F.
8. Sprinkle turkey with salt and black pepper evenly and stuff the cavity with garlic, lime, and lemon.
9. Arrange the turkey in a big roasting pan and roast for approximately a half-hour.
10. Now, reduce the temperature of the oven to 350 degrees F.
11. Roast for around 3 hours. (if skin becomes brown during roasting, then cover with foil paper)

Nutrition:

- Calories: 434,
- Fat: 12g,
- Carbohydrates: 20g,
- Fiber: 3g,
- Protein: 39g

GRILLED TURKEY BREAST

Preparation Time: 15 minutes

Cooking Time: 6-10 minutes

Serving: 4

Ingredients:

1 large shallot, quartered

(¾-inch) piece fresh ginger, chopped

2 small garlic cloves, chopped

1 tablespoon honey

¼ cup extra virgin olive oil

¼ cup coconut aminos

2 tablespoons fresh lime juice

Freshly ground black pepper, to taste

4 turkey breast tenderloins

Directions:

1. In a food processor, add shallot, ginger, and garlic and pulse till minced.
2. Add remaining ingredients except for turkey tenderloins and pulse till well combined.
3. Transfer the mixture to a sizable bowl.
4. Add turkey tenderloins and coat with mixture generously.
5. Keep aside, covered for approximately 30 minutes.
6. Preheat the grill to medium heat. Grease the grill grate.
7. Grill for about 6-8 minutes per side.

Nutrition:

- Calories: 412,
- Fat: 14g,
- Carbohydrates: 17g,
- Fiber: 3g,
- Protein: 38g

DUCK WITH BOK CHOY

Preparation Time: 15 minutes

Cooking Time: 12 minutes

Serving: 4-6

Ingredients:

2 tablespoons coconut oil

1 onion, sliced thinly

2 teaspoons fresh ginger, grated finely

2 minced garlic cloves

1 tablespoon fresh orange zest, grated finely

¼ cup chicken broth

2/3 cup fresh lime juice

1 roasted duck, meat picked

3-pound Bok choy leaves

1 lemon, peeled, seeded, and segmented

Directions:

1. In a sizable skillet, melt coconut oil on medium heat.
2. Add onion, ginger, and garlic and sauté for around 3 minutes.
3. Add ginger and garlic and sauté for about 1-2 minutes.
4. Stir in orange zest, broth, and lime juice.
5. Add duck meat and cook for around 3 minutes.
6. Transfer the meat pieces to a plate.
7. Add Bok choy and cook for about 3-4 minutes.
8. Divide Bok choy mixture in serving plates and top with duck meat.
9. Serve with the garnishing.

Nutrition:

- Calories: 433,
- Fat: 12g,
- Carbohydrates: 21g,
- Fiber: 9g,
- Protein: 34g

GRILLED DUCK BREAST & PEACH

Preparation Time: 15 minutes

Cooking Time: 24 minutes

Serving: 2

Ingredients:

2 shallots, sliced thinly

2 tablespoons fresh ginger, minced

2 tablespoons fresh thyme, chopped

Salt and freshly ground black pepper, to taste

2 duck breasts

2 peaches, pitted and quartered

½ teaspoon ground fennel seeds

½ tablespoon extra-virgin olive oil

Directions:

1. In a substantial bowl, mix shallots, ginger, thyme, salt, and black pepper.
2. Add duck breasts and coat with marinade evenly.
3. Refrigerate to marinate for about 2-12 hours.
4. Preheat the grill to medium-high heat. Grease the grill grate.
5. In a sizable bowl, add peaches, fennel seeds, salt, black pepper, and oil and toss to coat well.
6. Place the duck breast on the grill, skin side down, and grill for around 6-8 minutes per side.
7. Transfer the duck breast onto a plate.
8. Now, grill the peaches for around 3 minutes per side.
9. Serve the duck breasts with grilled peaches.

Nutrition:

- Calories: 450,
- Fat: 14g,
- Carbohydrates: 25g,
- Fiber: 12g,
- Protein: 42g

SLOW COOKER TURKEY LEGS

Preparation Time: 15 minutes

Cooking Time: 20 minutes

Serving: 2

Ingredients:

2 turkey legs

1 tablespoon mustard

1 tablespoon butter

1/2 teaspoon smoked paprika

1 teaspoon dried rosemary

Salt and pepper, to taste

1 chopped leek

1/2 teaspoon minced garlic

For the Gravy:

1/2 stick butter

1 cup heavy cream

Salt and pepper, to taste

Directions:

1. Rub turkey legs with the mustard and butter.
2. Preheat a skillet over medium-high heat Fry the turkey legs on all sides, making sure that they are brown all over.
3. Put the turkey legs in the slow cooker but keep the fat to one side. Add the paprika, rosemary, pepper, salt, leeks, and garlic.
4. Put the slow cooker on low and cook for 6 hours.
5. Heat the reserved fat with 1/2 stick of butter on a medium flame. Add the cream to the fat and stir until the mixture is hot.
6. Add salt and pepper and stir until the sauce is thickened and hot. Serve the sauce on top of the chicken drumsticks. Enjoy.

Nutrition:

- Calories 280,
- Protein 15.8g,
- Fat 22.2g,
- Carbs 4.3g,
- Sugar 1.7g

TURKEY AND CAULIFLOWER SOUP

Preparation Time: 15 minutes

Cooking Time: 20 minutes

Serving: 2

Ingredients:

2 tablespoons coconut oil

2 chopped garlic cloves

2 chopped shallots

4 ½ cups chicken stock

1/2 head cauliflower florets

1 pound turkey thighs

2 bay leaves

1 rosemary sprig

1/2 teaspoon celery seeds

Salt and ground black pepper, to taste

1/2 teaspoon cayenne pepper

4 dollops of sour cream

Directions:

1. Preheat a heavy pot over a medium flame and heat the oil. Sauté the garlic and shallots until they are fragrant.
2. Pour in the chicken stock and bring to the boil.
3. Add the turkey, cauliflower, bay leaves, celery seeds, rosemary, salt, pepper, and cayenne pepper.
4. Simmer on a moderate-low heat for 25 – 30 minutes.
5. Pour the soup into 4 bowls and put a dollop of sour cream on each Enjoy!

Nutrition:

- Calories274,
- Protein 26.7g,
- Fat 14.4g,
- Carbs 5.6g,
- Sugar 3.1g

CHICKEN LEFTOVERS CHOWDER

Preparation Time: 15 minutes

Cooking Time: 30 minutes

Serving: 2

Ingredients:

2 tablespoons coconut oil

2 roughly chopped cloves of garlic

A bunch of chopped scallions

1/2 pound shredded and skinned leftover roast chicken

2 rosemary sprigs

1 bay leaf

1 thyme sprig

1 tablespoon chicken bouillon granules

3 cups water

1/2 cup whipped cream

1 1/2 cups milk

1 lightly beaten whole egg

1 tablespoon dry sherry

Directions:s

1. Preheat a stockpot over a moderate flame and melt the coconut oil. Sauté the garlic and scallions until softened and fragrant.

2. Add the chicken, rosemary, bay leaf, thyme, chicken bouillon granules, and water. Partially cover and bring to the boil. Then simmer for 20 minutes.

3. Turn the heat down to low and add the whipped cream and milk. Simmer until it has thickened. Put in the egg and stir for a couple of minutes.

4. Taste to make sure the seasoning is right. Ladle into individual bowls and drizzle each with the sherry. Enjoy!

Nutrition:

- Calories350,
- Protein 20g,
- Fat 25.8g,
- Carbs 5.5g,
- Sugar 2.8g

Preparation Time: 15 minutes

Cooking Time: 30 minutes

Serving: 2

Ingredients:

1 1/2 pounds diced British turkey thigh

2 tablespoons butter, at room temperature

1 tablespoon dry ranch seasoning

1 red onion, cut into wedges

1 sliced zucchini

2 sliced orange bell peppers

1 sliced red bell pepper

1 sliced green bell pepper

1 cup sliced radishes

1 sliced cucumber

2 tablespoons red wine vinegar

1 tablespoon roughly chopped fresh parsley

Directions:

1. Rub the butter on the turkey and then add the seasoning. Put the turkey pieces on skewers.
2. Alternate the onion, zucchini, and bell peppers on the skewers and put them in the fridge while you get the grill ready.
3. Put the kebabs on the grill and cook for 9 minutes, turning now and then.
4. While they are cooking mix the radishes and cucumbers with the parsley and red wine vinegar.
5. Serve the kebabs with the salad straight away and enjoy!

Nutrition:

- Calories 293,
- Protein 34.5g,
- Fat 13.8g,
- Carbs 3.7g,

- Sugar 1.9g

BAKED EGGPLANT TURKEY

Preparation time: 10 minutes

Cooking Time: 50 minutes

Serving: 6-8

Ingredients:

½ cup green pepper, chopped

½ cup onion, finely chopped

1 large eggplant

2 tablespoons vegetable oil

2 cups plain bread crumbs

1 large egg, slightly beaten

1 pound lean ground turkey

½ teaspoon red pepper, optional

Directions:

1. Preheat an oven to 350°F. Grease a casserole dish with some cooking spray.
2. In boiling water, cook eggplant until fully tender.
3. Drain and mash eggplant well.
4. Take a medium saucepan or skillet, add oil. Heat over medium heat.
5. Add onion, green pepper, and stir-cook until it becomes translucent and softened.
6. Add ground meat and stir-cook until evenly brown.
7. Mix in eggplant, egg, and bread crumbs. Season to taste with red pepper.
8. Add the mixture to a casserole dish and bake for 35-45 minutes until meat is cooked to satisfaction.
9. Serve warm.

Nutrition:

- Calories: 263
- Fat: 7g

- Phosphorus: 162mg
- Potassium: 373mg
- Sodium: 281mg
- Carbohydrates: 4g
- Protein: 14g

Preparation time: 10 minutes

Cooking Time: 45 minutes

Serving: 6-8

Ingredients:

½ teaspoon Italian seasoning

¼ teaspoon black pepper

½ teaspoon onion powder

½ cup chopped onions

1-pound lean ground turkey

1 egg white

1 tablespoon lemon juice

½ cup plain bread crumbs

½ cup diced green bell pepper

¼ cup of water

Directions:

1. Preheat an oven to 400°F. Grease a baking dish with some cooking spray.
2. In a mixing bowl, add turkey and lemon juice. Combine to mix well with each other.
3. Add other ingredients and combine well.
4. Add the mixture to a baking dish and bake for 40-45 minutes until cooked to satisfaction.
5. Serve warm.

Nutrition:

- Calories: 123
- Fat: 6g

- Phosphorus: 94mg
- Potassium: 142mg
- Sodium: 83mg
- Carbohydrates: 9g
- Protein: 13g

Coconut Chicken Curry

Preparation time: 10 minutes

Cooking Time:40 minutes

Serving: 6

Ingredients:

1 small sweet onion

2 teaspoons minced garlic

1 teaspoon grated ginger

3 tablespoons olive oil

6 boneless, skinless chicken thighs

1 tablespoon curry powder

¾ cup of water

¼ cup of coconut milk

2 tablespoons cilantro, chopped

Directions:

1. Take a medium saucepan or skillet, add 2 tablespoons of oil. Heat over medium heat.
2. Add chicken and stir-cook until evenly brown, about 8-10 minutes. Set aside.
3. Add remaining oil. Add onion, ginger, garlic, and stir-cook until become softened, about3-4 minutes.
4. Mix in curry powder, water, and coconut milk. Add chicken, stir the mixture and boil it.
5. Over low heat, cover, and simmer the mixture for about 25 minutes until chicken is tender.
6. Serve warm with cilantro on top.

Nutrition:

- Calories: 258
- Fat: 13g
- Phosphorus: 151mg
- Potassium: 242mg
- Sodium: 86mg
- Carbohydrates: 2g
- Protein: 25g

JALAPENO CHICKEN DELIGHT

Preparation time: 10 minutes

Cooking Time: 30-35 minutes

Serving: 7-8

Ingredients:

1 ½ cups chicken stock

½ teaspoon ground nutmeg

¼ teaspoon black pepper

3 tablespoons vegetable oil

2-3 pounds skinless chicken, cut up and trimmed of fat

1 onion, sliced into rings

2 teaspoons jalapeño peppers, seeded and finely chopped

Directions:

1. Take a medium saucepan or skillet, add oil. Heat over medium heat.
2. Add chicken and stir-cook until evenly brown. Set aside.
3. Add onion rings and stir-cook until they become translucent and softened.
4. Pour chicken stock and boil the mixture.
5. Add cooked chicken pieces, nutmeg, and black pepper. Stir mixture.
6. Over medium-low heat, cover, and simmer the mixture for about 30-35 minutes until chicken is tender.
7. Add jalapeno pepper and simmer for 1 minute.

8. Serve warm.

Nutrition:

- Calories: 153
- Fat: 8g
- Phosphorus: 135mg
- Potassium: 171mg
- Sodium: 56mg
- Carbohydrates: 3g
- Protein: 17g

CLASSIC CHICKEN RICE

Preparation time: 10 minutes

Cooking Time: 20-25 minutes

Serving: 6-7

Ingredients:

1 teaspoon onion powder

½ teaspoon garlic powder

½ cup chopped onion

1 pound chicken parts

1 teaspoon black pepper

1 tablespoon poultry seasoning

4 cups of water

1 cup uncooked rice

1 tablespoon vegetable oil

1 teaspoon crushed bay leaves (optional)

Directions:

1. Take a medium-large cooking pot or Dutch oven, heat water over medium heat.
2. Add the chicken pieces, spring onions, onion powder, black pepper, poultry seasoning, bay leaves, and stir-cook until chicken is tender.
3. Take out the chicken, remove the skin from the bone. Take out 2 cups of cooking liquid.

4. In another large cooking, heat oil and reserved cooking liquid over medium heat.
5. Add chicken and rice. Stir mixture.
6. Over low heat simmer the mixture for about 20-25 minutes until rice is cooked well.
7. Serve warm.

Nutrition:
- Calories: 233
- Fat: 7g
- Phosphorus: 233mg
- Potassium: 291mg
- Sodium: 87mg
- Carbohydrates: 11g
- Protein: 22g

GRILLED CHICKEN PIZZA

Preparation time: 10 minutes

Cooking Time: 20-25 minutes

Serving: 6-7

Ingredients:

2 pita bread

3 tbsp. low sodium BBQ sauce

1/4 bowl red onion

4 oz. cooked chicken

2 tbsp. crumbled feta cheese

1/8 tsp. garlic powder

Directions:
1. Preheat oven at 350°F (that is 175° C).
2. Place 2 pitas on the pan after you have put nonstick cooking spray on it.
3. Spread BBQ sauce (2 tablespoons) on the pita.
4. Cut the onion and put it on pita. Cube chicken and put it on the pitas.

5. Put also both feta and the garlic powder over the pita.

6. Bake for 12 minutes. Serve and enjoy!

Nutrition:
- Calories: 320
- Protein: 22 g
- Sodium: 520 mg
- Potassium: 250 mg
- Phosphorus: 220 mg

CHICKEN BREAST AND BOK CHOY

Preparation time: 10 minutes

Cooking Time: 30minutes

Serving: 6-7

Ingredients:

4 slices lemon

Pepper, to taste

4 chicken breasts, boneless and skinless

1 tbsp. Dijon mustard

1 small leek, thinly sliced

2 julienned carrots

2 cups thinly sliced bok choy

1 tbsp. chopped thyme

1 tbsp. EVOO

Directions:

1. Start by setting your oven to 425 F.

2. Mix the thyme, olive oil, and mustard in a small bowl.

3. Take four 18-inch-long pieces of parchment paper and fold them in half. Cut them like you would make a heart. Open each of the pieces and lay them flat.

4. In each parchment piece, place .5 cup of bok choy, a few slices of leek, and a small handful of carrots.

5. Lay the chicken breast on top and season with some pepper.

6. Brush the chicken breasts with the marinade and top each one with a slice of lemon.
7. Fold the packets up and roll down the edges to seal the packages.
8. Allow them to cook for 20 minutes. Let them rest for 5 minutes, and make sure you open them carefully when serving. Enjoy!

Nutrition:
- Calories: 164
- Protein: 24 g
- Sodium: 356 mg
- Potassium: 189 mg
- Phosphorus: 26 mg

BAKED HERBED CHICKEN

Preparation time: 10 minutes

Cooking Time: 30minutes

Serving: 4

Ingredients:

1/4 tsp. pepper

6 chicken thighs, bone-in

1 tbsp. chopped oregano

1 tsp. lemon zest

1 tbsp. chopped parsley

4 garlic cloves, minced

4 tbsp. butter at room temperature

Directions:
1. Start by setting your oven to 425 F.
2. Add the lemon zest, parsley, oregano, garlic, and butter to a small bowl and mix well, making sure that everything is distributed evenly throughout the butter.
3. Lay the chicken on a baking pan and gently pull the skin back, but leaving it attached.
4. Brush the thigh meat with some of the butter mixtures and lay the skin back over the meat. Sprinkle on some pepper.

5. Bake the chicken for 40 minutes. The skin should be crispy, and the juices should be clear. Also, the chicken should reach 165 F.
6. Allow the chicken to rest for 5 minutes before serving. Enjoy!

Nutrition:

- Calories: 226
- Protein: 16 g
- Sodium: 120 mg
- Potassium: 158 mg
- Phosphorus: 114 mg

BRAISED CARROTS 'N KALE

Preparation Time: 10 minutes

Cooking Time: 10 minutes

Serving: 2

Ingredients:

1 tablespoon coconut oil

1 onion, sliced thinly

5 cloves of garlic, minced

3 medium carrots, sliced thinly

10 ounces of kale, chopped

½ cup water

Salt and pepper to taste

A dash of red pepper flakes

Directions:

1. Heat oil in a skillet over medium flame and sauté the onion and garlic until fragrant.
2. Toss in the carrots and stir for 1 minute. Add the kale and water. Season with salt and pepper to taste.
3. Close the lid and allow to simmer for 5 minutes.
4. Sprinkle with red pepper flakes.
5. Serve and enjoy.

Nutrition:

- Calories 161,

- Total Fat 8g,
- Saturated Fat 1g,
- Total Carbs 20g,
- Net Carbs 14g,
- Protein 8g,
- Sugar: 6g,
- Fiber 6g,
- Sodium 63mg,
- Potassium 900mg

EGGPLANT HUMMUS

Preparation Time: 10 minutes

Cooking Time: 15 minutes

Serving: 8

Ingredients:

1 1/2 lbs Eggplant

1 tablespoon olive oil

3-4 Large Cloves of Garlic

¼ cup tahini

2 cups Cooked Chickpeas, drained

2 tablespoons lemon juice

2 cloves of garlic, minced

Salt and pepper to taste

Directions:

1. Preheat oven to 450F (232C) and line a baking tray with parchment paper. Cut eggplant in half lengthwise and score the flesh.
2. Drizzle olive oil on top of the halved eggplant. Place. Sole garlic on top of the tray as well.
3. Roast the garlic and eggplant for about 30 minutes, until soft.
4. Remove from oven and remove the skin.

5. Once soft and pealed, place the aubergines and garlic in a food processor together with the rest of the ingredients.
6. Pulse until smooth.
7. Place in individual containers.
8. Put a label and store it in the fridge.
9. Allow warming at room temperature before heating in the microwave oven.
10. Serve with carrots or celery sticks.

Nutrition:

- Calories 109,
- Total Fat 6g,
- Saturated Fat 0.8g,
- Total Carbs 15g,
- Net Carbs 11g,
- Protein 2g,
- Sugar: 3g,
- Fiber 4g,
- Sodium 14mg,
- Potassium 379mg

STIR-FRIED GINGERY VEGGIES

Preparation Time: 10 minutes

Cooking Time: 10 minutes

Serving: 4

Ingredients:

1 tablespoon oil

3 cloves of garlic, minced

1 onion, chopped

1 thumb-size ginger, sliced

1 tablespoon water

1 large carrot, peeled and julienned

1 large green bell pepper, seeded and julienned

1 large yellow bell pepper, seeded and julienned

1 large red bell pepper, seeded and julienned

1 zucchini, julienned

Salt and pepper to taste

Directions:

- Heat oil in a nonstick saucepan over a high flame and sauté the garlic, onion, and ginger until fragrant.
- Stir in the rest of the ingredients.
- Keep on stirring for at least 5 minutes until vegetables are tender.
- Serve and enjoy.

Nutrition:

- Calories 70,
- Total Fat 4g,
- Saturated Fat 1g,
- Total Carbs 9g,
- Net Carbs 7g,
- Protein 1g,
- Sugar: 4g,
- Fiber 2g,
- Sodium 273mg,
- Potassium 263mg

STIR-FRIED ZUCCHINI

Preparation Time: 10 minutes

Cooking Time: 10 minutes

Serving: 4

Ingredients:

1 tablespoon olive oil

3 cloves of garlic, minced

10 zucchini, seeded and sliced

1 tablespoon coconut aminos

1 tablespoon lemon juice

1 tablespoon water

Salt and pepper to taste

Directions:

1. Heat oil over medium flame and sauté the garlic until fragrant.
2. Stir in the zucchini for another 3 minutes before adding the rest of the ingredients.
3. Close the lid and allow to simmer for 5 more minutes or until zucchini are soft.
4. Serve and enjoy.

Nutrition:

- Calories 83,
- Total Fat 3g,
- Saturated Fat 0.5g,
- Total Carbs 14g,
- Net Carbs 12g,
- Protein 2g,
- Sugar: 1g,
- Fiber 2g,
- Sodium 8mg,
- Potassium 211mg

CARROT PUREE

Preparation Time: 10 minutes

Cooking Time: 15 minutes

Serving: 6

Ingredients:

1 pound carrots, peeled

1 pound potatoes, peeled

1 cups water

1 tablespoon honey

Directions:

1. Place water carrots and potatoes in a pot.
2. Close the lid and allow to boil for 15 minutes until the potatoes are soft.

3. Drain the potatoes and the carrots and place them in a food processor together with honey.
4. Pulse until smooth.
5. Serve and enjoy.

Nutrition:
- Calories 172,
- Total Fat 0.2g,
- Saturated Fat 0g,
- Total Carbs 41g,
- Net Carbs 36g,
- Protein 3g,
- Sugar: 14g,
- Fiber 5g,
- Sodium 10mg,
- Potassium 776mg

CURRIED OKRA

Preparation Time: 10 minutes

Cooking Time: 12 minutes

Serving: 4

Ingredients:

1 lb. small to medium okra pods, trimmed

¼ tsp curry powder

½ tsp kosher salt

1 tsp finely chopped serrano chile

1 tsp ground coriander

1 tbsp canola oil

¾ tsp brown mustard seeds

Directions:
1. On medium-high fire, place a large and heavy skillet and cook mustard seeds until fragrant, around 30 seconds.
2. Add canola oil. Add okra, curry powder, salt, chile, and coriander. Sauté for a minute while stirring every once in a while.

3. Cover and cook low fire for at least 8 minutes. Stir occasionally.
4. Uncover, increase the fire to medium-high and cook until okra is lightly browned, around 2 minutes more.
5. Serve and enjoy.

Nutrition:

- Calories 78,
- Total Fat 6g,
- Saturated Fat 0.7g,
- Total Carbs 6g,
- Net Carbs 3g,
- Protein 2g,
- Sugar: 3g,
- Fiber 3g,
- Sodium 553mg,
- Potassium 187mg

ZUCCHINI PASTA WITH MANGO-PINEAPPLE SAUCE

Preparation Time: 10 minutes

Cooking Time: 0 minutes

Serving: 2

Ingredients:

1 tsp dried herbs – optional

½ Cup Raw Kale leaves, shredded

2 small dried figs

4 slices pineapple

2 big mangos, peeled and seed discarded

2 cup zucchini, spiralized

¼ cup roasted cashew

Directions:

1. On a salad bowl, place kale then topped with zucchini noodles and sprinkle with dried herbs. Set aside.
2. In a food processor, grind to a powder the cashews. Add figs, pineapple, and mango then puree to a smooth consistency.

3. Pour over zucchini pasta, serve and enjoy.

Nutrition:

- Calories 370,
- Total Fat 9g,
- Saturated Fat 2g,
- Total Carbs 76g,
- Net Carbs 67g,
- Protein 6g,
- Sugar: 62g,
- Fiber 9g,
- Sodium 8mg,
- Potassium 868mg

Chapter 4

Dinner Recipes

TOFU STIR FRY

Preparation Time: 15 minutes

Cooking Time: 20 minutes

Serving: 4

Ingredients:

1 teaspoon sugar

1 tablespoon lime juice

1 tablespoon low sodium soy sauce

2 tablespoons cornstarch

2 egg whites, beaten

1/2 cup unseasoned breadcrumbs

1 tablespoon vegetable oil

16 ounces tofu, cubed

1 clove garlic, minced

1 tablespoon sesame oil

1 red bell pepper, sliced into strips

1 cup eggplants

1 teaspoon herb seasoning blend

Dash black pepper

Sesame seeds

Steamed white rice

Directions:

1. Dissolve sugar in a mixture of lime juice and soy sauce. Set aside.
2. In the first bowl, put the cornstarch.
3. Add the egg whites to the second bowl.
4. Place the breadcrumbs in the third bowl.
5. Dip each tofu cubes in the first, second, and third bowls.
6. Pour vegetable oil into a pan over medium heat.
7. Cook tofu cubes until golden.
8. Drain the tofu and set aside.
9. Remove the oil from the pan and add sesame oil.
10. Add garlic, bell pepper, and eggplants.
11. Cook until crisp-tender.
12. Season with the seasoning blend and pepper.
13. Put the tofu back and toss to mix.
14. Pour soy sauce mixture on top and transfer to serving bowls.
15. Garnish with the sesame seeds and serve on top of white rice.

Nutrition:

- Calories 400
- Protein 19 g
- Carbohydrates 45 g
- Fat 16 g
- Cholesterol 0 mg
- Sodium 584 mg
- Potassium 317 mg

- Phosphorus 177 mg
- Calcium 253 mg
- Fiber 2.7 g

ZUCCHINI PANCAKE

Preparation Time: 10 minutes

Cooking Time: 5 minutes

Serving: 4

Ingredients:

3 cups zucchini, diced

2 eggs, beaten

2 tablespoons all-purpose flour

½ cup onion, chopped

2 tablespoons olive oil

Directions:

1. Stir fry zucchini in a pan for 1o to 15 minutes. Drain and set aside.
2. Mix egg and flour.
3. Add onion and zucchini to the mixture.
4. Pour oil into a pan over medium heat.
5. Cook the zucchini pancake until brown on both sides.

Nutrition:

- Calories 140
- Protein 6 g
- Carbohydrates 7 g
- Fat 10 g
- Cholesterol 106 mg
- Sodium 58 mg
- Potassium 276 mg
- Phosphorus 101 mg
- Calcium 50 mg
- Fiber 2.1 g

Preparation Time: 10 minutes

Cooking Time: 20 minutes

Serving: 8

Ingredients:

1 lb. carrots, sliced into rounds

12 low-sodium crackers

2 tablespoons butter

2 tablespoons onion, chopped

1/4 cup Swiss cheese, shredded

Directions:

1. Preheat your oven to 350 degrees F.
2. Boil carrots in a pot of water until tender.
3. Drain the carrots and reserve ¼ cup liquid.
4. Mash carrots.
5. Add all the ingredients into the carrots except cheese.
6. Place the mashed carrots in a casserole dish.
7. Sprinkle cheese on top and bake in the oven for 15 minutes.

Nutrition:

*   Calories 94
*   Protein 2 g
*   Carbohydrates 9 g
*   Fat 6 g
*   Cholesterol 13 mg
*   Sodium 174 mg
*   Potassium 153 mg
*   Phosphorus 47 mg
*   Calcium 66 mg
*   Fiber 1.8 g

Preparation Time: 10 minutes

Cooking Time: 10 minutes

Serving: 4

Ingredients:

1 head cauliflower, sliced into florets

1 tablespoon butter

Black pepper to taste

1/4 teaspoon garlic powder

1/4 teaspoon herb seasoning blend

Directions:

1. Put cauliflower florets in a food processor.
2. Pulse until consistency is similar to grain.
3. In a pan over medium heat, melt the butter and add the spices.
4. Toss cauliflower rice and cook for 10 minutes.
5. Fluff using a fork before serving.

Nutrition:

- Calories 47
- Protein 1 g
- Carbohydrates 4 g
- Fat 3 g
- Cholesterol 8 mg
- Sodium 43 mg
- Potassium 206 mg
- Phosphorus 31 mg
- Calcium 16 mg
- Fiber 1.4 g

CHICKEN PINEAPPLE CURRY

Preparation Time: 10 minutes

Cooking Time: 5 minutes

Serving: 4

Ingredients:

1 1/2 lbs. chicken thighs, boneless, skinless

1/2 teaspoon black pepper

1/2 teaspoon garlic powder

2 tablespoons olive oil

20 oz. canned pineapple

2 tablespoons brown Swerve

2 tablespoons low-sodium soy sauce

1/2 teaspoon Tabasco sauce

2 tablespoons cornstarch

3 tablespoons water

Directions:

1. Begin by seasoning the chicken thighs with garlic powder and black pepper.
2. Set a suitable skillet over medium-high heat and add the oil to heat.
3. Add the boneless chicken to the skillet and cook for 3 minutes per side.
4. Transfer this seared chicken to a Slow cooker, greased with cooking spray.
5. Add 1 cup of the pineapple juice, Swerve, 1 cup of pineapple, tabasco sauce, and soy sauce to a slow cooker.
6. Cover the chicken-pineapple mixture and cook for 3 hours on low heat.
7. Transfer the chicken to the serving plates.
8. Mix the cornstarch with water in a small bowl and pour it into the pineapple curry.
9. Stir and cook this sauce for 2 minutes on high heat until it thickens.
10. Pour this sauce over the chicken and garnish with green onions.
11. Serve warm.

Nutrition:

- Calories 256

- Total Fat 10.4g
- Saturated Fat 2.2g
- Cholesterol 67mg
- Sodium 371mg
- Total Carbohydrate 13.6g
- Dietary Fiber 1.5g
- Sugars 8.4g
- Protein 22.8g
- Calcium 28mg
- Phosphorous 107 mg
- Potassium 308mg

BAKED PORK CHOPS

Preparation Time: 10 minutes

Cooking Time: 30 minutes

Serving: 4

Ingredients:

1/2 cup flour

1 large egg

1/4 cup water

3/4 cup breadcrumbs

6 (3 1/2 oz.) pork chops

2 tablespoons butter, unsalted

1 teaspoon paprika

Directions:

1. Begin by switching the oven to 350 degrees F to preheat.
2. Mix and spread the flour on a shallow plate.
3. Whisk the egg with water in another shallow bowl.
4. Spread the breadcrumbs on a separate plate.
5. Firstly, coat the pork with flour, then dip in the egg mix and then in the crumbs.
6. Grease a baking sheet and place the chops in it.
7. Drizzle the pepper on top and bake for 40 minutes.

8. Serve.

Nutrition:

- Calories 221
- Total Fat 7.8g
- Saturated Fat 1.9g
- Cholesterol 93mg
- Sodium 135mg
- Carbohydrate 11.9g
- Dietary Fiber 3.5g
- Sugars 0.5g
- Protein 24.7g
- Calcium 13mg
- Phosphorous 299mg
- Potassium 391mg

LASAGNA ROLLS IN MARINARA SAUCE

Preparation Time: 10 minutes

Cooking Time: 40 minutes

Serving: 4

Ingredients:

¼ tsp crushed red pepper

¼ tsp salt

½ cup shredded mozzarella cheese

½ cups parmesan cheese, shredded

1 14-oz package tofu, cubed

1 25-oz can of low-sodium marinara sauce

1 tbsp extra virgin olive oil

12 lasagna noodles

2 tbsp Kalamata olives, chopped

3 cloves minced garlic

3 cups spinach, chopped

Directions:

1. Put enough water on a large pot and cook the lasagna noodles according to package directions. Drain, rinse, and set aside until ready to use.

2. In a large skillet, sauté garlic over medium heat for 20 seconds. Add the tofu and spinach and cook until the spinach wilts. Transfer this mixture to a bowl and add parmesan olives, salt, red pepper, and 2/3 cup of the marinara sauce.

3. In a pan, spread a cup of marinara sauce on the bottom. To make the rolls, place noodle on a surface and spread ¼ cup of the tofu filling. Roll up and place it on the pan with the marinara sauce. Do this procedure until all lasagna noodles are rolled.

4. Place the pan over high heat and bring to a simmer. Reduce the heat to medium and let it cook for three more minutes. Sprinkle mozzarella cheese and let the cheese melt for two minutes. Serve hot.

Nutrition:

- Calories: 600;
- Carbs: 65g;
- Protein: 36g;
- Fats: 26g;
- Phosphorus: 627mg;
- Potassium: 914mg;
- Sodium: 1194mg

BAKED HERBED CHICKEN

Preparation Time: 10 minutes

Cooking Time: 30 minutes

Serving: 4

Ingredients:

1/2 pound skinless & boneless chicken breasts, or 3/4 pound chicken with bone

1 slice whole-wheat bread

1/4 teaspoon fresh thyme

1/4 teaspoon fresh basil

1/4 teaspoon fresh ground black pepper

1/4 teaspoon fresh tarragon

1/4 teaspoon fresh paprika

1/4 teaspoon fresh oregano

Directions:

1. Turn up your oven to 400 F (about 200 C) and preheat for about 10 to 20 minutes.
2. In the jar of a blender or a food processor, place the whole wheat bread, thyme, basil, ground black pepper, tarragon, paprika, and oregano.
3. Blitz until well combined.
4. Dunk the chicken in a bowl of chilled water and immediately dip it in the bread, herb, and spice mix.
5. Grease a shallow baking dish with some oil and place the herb-crusted chicken in the baking dish.
6. Pop the baking dish into the preheated oven and bake for about 25 to 30 minutes (if using boneless chicken) or about 55 minutes to an hour (if using chicken with bone).
7. Remove from the oven and allow the chicken to rest for a few minutes.
8. Serve hot with a side of boiled vegetables and a sauce of your choice.
9. Enjoy!

Nutrition:

- Protein 26.51g (49%),
- Potassium (K) 815 mg (17%) and
- Sodium, Na 215 mg (14%)

Preparation Time: 10 minutes

Cooking Time: 30 minutes

Serving: 4

Ingredients:

2 medium green bell peppers

1 teaspoon oregano leaves, finely chopped

1/2 tablespoon balsamic vinegar

1/2 cup goat cheese, crumbled

Ground black pepper, to taste

2 teaspoons olive oil

4 slices French bread, toasted

Directions:

1. Chop the green pepper into ½ inch thick slices.
2. Pour a little olive oil into a shallow baking dish and swivel it around so that the baking dish is well coated with oil.
3. Place the bell pepper slices in a single overlapping layer in the bottom of the greased baking dish.
4. Drizzle the vinegar over the bell pepper slices and sprinkle the finely chopped oregano over them.
5. Add the crumbled goat cheese and drizzle the remaining olive oil over the goat cheese.
6. Place the baking dish in a preheated oven and broil about 5 to 8 inches below the broiler, for about 8 to10 minutes or until the bell peppers get hot and the cheese has melted and starts to brown around the edges.
7. Remove the baking dish from the oven and allow it to cool for a few minutes. Carefully spoon out the prepared bell pepper and cheese and place it on the toasted bread. Sprinkle some pepper over it.
8. Serve immediately.
9. Enjoy!

Nutrition:

- Protein 26.51g (49%),
- Potassium (K) 815 mg (17%) and
- Sodium, Na 215 mg (14%)

Preparation Time: 10 minutes

Cooking Time: 30 minutes

Serving: 4

Ingredients:

2 cups rice vermicelli

4 oz cooked beef

2 oz frozen prawns, thawed

4 tablespoons vegetable oil

1 onion, shredded

2 cups bean sprouts

1 teaspoon salt

1 tablespoon curry powder

2 tablespoons low-sodium soy sauce

2 green or red chili peppers

2 spring onions, shredded

Directions:

1. Soak rice vermicelli in boiling water for 10 minutes. Rinse in cold water.
2. Slice beef meat thinly. Dry prawns in a paper towel.
3. Heat oil in a wok. Stir fry onion and beans for 2 minutes.
4. Add noodles, beef, and prawns. Stir for 3 minutes.
5. Tip in curry powder, soy sauce, chili peppers, and spring onions. Stir fry for 1 minute. Serve.

Nutrition:

- Protein 14.3g (26%),
- Potassium (K) 460 mg (10%) and
- Sodium, Na 888 mg (59%),

- Content of Sodium without added salt 307mg (20%)

Preparation Time: 10 minutes

Cooking Time: 0 minutes

Serving: 4

Ingredients:

1 1/2 cup watermelon, chopped into bite-sized chunks, seeds removed

1 tablespoon lime juice

1/2 cup green bell pepper, finely chopped

1/2 tablespoon cilantro, finely chopped

1 medium jalapeno, cut lengthwise, seeds removed and minced

1/2 tablespoon green onion, chopped

1 garlic clove, crushed

Directions:

1. In a large mixing bowl combine the watermelon chunks, green bell pepper, jalapeno, green onion, and garlic. Mix well.
2. Pour the lemon juice over the prepared salad and toss well to coat.
3. Cover the bowl with a cling film and refrigerate for at least 2 hours.
4. Serve chilled topped with cilantro.
5. Enjoy!

Nutrition:

- Protein 26.51g (49%),
- Potassium (K) 815 mg (17%) and
- Sodium, Na 215 mg (14%)

Preparation time: 10 minutes

Cooking Time: 40-45 minutes

Serving: 4

Ingredients:

1 teaspoon black pepper

½ teaspoon sage

½ teaspoon thyme

2 tablespoons vegetable oil

¼ cup all-purpose flour

4 4-ounce lean pork chops (fat removed)

Directions:

1. Preheat an oven to 350^{0}F.Grease a baking pan with some vegetable oil.

2. In a mixing bowl, add flour, thyme, sage, and black pepper. Combine to mix well with each other.

3. Add pork chops and coat well.

4. Place over a baking pan and bake for 40-45 minutes until cooked perfectly and evenly brown.

5. Serve warm.

Nutrition:

- Calories: 421
- Fat: 23g
- Phosphorus: 204mg
- Potassium: 328mg
- Sodium: 81mg
- Carbohydrates: 13g
- Protein: 19g

STEAK BURGERS/SANDWICH

Preparation time: 10 minutes

Cooking Time:8-10 minutes

Serving: 4

Ingredients:

1 tablespoon lemon juice

1 tablespoon Italian seasoning

1 teaspoon black pepper

4 flank steaks (around 4 oz. each)

1 medium red onion, sliced

1 tablespoon vegetable oil

4 sandwich/burger buns

Directions:

1. Season steaks with lemon juice, Italian seasoning, and black pepper.
2. Take a medium saucepan or skillet, add oil. Heat over medium heat.
3. Add steaks and stir-cook for 5-6 minutes until evenly brown. Set aside.
4. Add onion and stir cook for 2-3 minutes until it becomes translucent and softened.
5. Slice burger buns into half and place 1 steak piece over.
6. Add onion mixture on top. Add another bun piece on top and serve fresh.

Nutrition:

- Calories: 349
- Fat: 12g
- Phosphorus: 312mg
- Potassium: 241mg
- Sodium: 287mg
- Carbohydrates: 9g
- Protein: 36g

HEARTY MEATLOAF

Preparation time: 10 minutes

Cooking Time: 45-50 minutes

Serving: 7-8

Ingredients:

1 large egg

2 tablespoons chopped fresh basil

1 teaspoon chopped fresh thyme

1 teaspoon chopped fresh parsley

¼ teaspoon black pepper (ground)

1 pound 95% lean ground beef

½ cup bread crumbs

½ cup chopped sweet onion

1 teaspoon white vinegar

¼ teaspoon garlic powder

1 tablespoon brown sugar

Directions:

1. Preheat an oven to 350^{0}F.Grease a loaf pan (9X5-inch) with some cooking spray.
2. In a mixing bowl, add beef, bread crumbs, onion, egg, basil, thyme, parsley, and black pepper. Combine to mix well with each other.
3. Add the mixture to the pan.
4. Take another mixing bowl; add brown sugar, vinegar, and garlic powder. Combine to mix well with each other.
5. Add brown sugar mixture over the meat mixture.
6. Bake for about 50 minutes until golden brown.
7. Serve warm.

Nutrition:

- Calories: 118
- Fat: 3g
- Phosphorus: 127mg
- Potassium: 203mg
- Sodium: 106mg
- Carbohydrates: 8g
- Protein: 12g

FISH SHAKSHUKA

Preparation Time: 5 minutes

Cooking time: 15 minutes

Serving:5

Ingredients:

5 eggs

1 cup tomatoes, chopped

3 bell peppers, chopped

1 tablespoon butter

1 teaspoon tomato paste

1 teaspoon chili pepper

1 teaspoon salt

1 tablespoon fresh dill

5 oz cod fillet, chopped

1 tablespoon scallions, chopped

Directions:

1. Melt butter in the skillet and add chili pepper, bell peppers, and tomatoes.
2. Sprinkle the vegetables with scallions, dill, salt, and chili pepper. Simmer them for 5 minutes.
3. After this, add chopped cod fillet and mix up well.
4. Close the lid and simmer the ingredients for 5 minutes over medium heat.
5. Then crack the eggs over the fish and close the lid.
6. Cook shakshuka with the closed lid for 5 minutes.

Nutrition:

- Calories 143,
- Fat 7.3g,
- Fiber 1.6g,
- Carbs 7.9g,
- Protein 12.8g

MACKEREL SKILLET WITH GREENS

Preparation Time: 10 minutes

Cooking time: 15 minutes

Serving: 4

Ingredients:

1 cup fresh spinach, chopped

½ cup endive, chopped

11 oz mackerel

1 tablespoon olive oil

1 teaspoon ground nutmeg

½ teaspoon salt

½ teaspoon turmeric

½ teaspoon chili flakes

3 tablespoons sour cream

Directions:

1. Pour olive oil in the skillet.
2. Add mackerel and sprinkle it with chili flakes, turmeric, and salt.
3. Roast fish for 2 minutes from each side.
4. Then add chopped endive, fresh spinach, and sour cream.
5. Mix up well and close the lid.
6. Simmer the meat for 10 minutes over medium-low heat.

Nutrition:

- Calories 260,
- Fat 19.5g,
- Fiber 0.5g,
- Carbs 1.3g,
- Protein 19.2g

CATFISH BALLS WITH CREAM CHEESE

Preparation Time: 15 minutes

Cooking time: 15 minutes

Serving:5

Ingredients:

1-pound catfish fillet

2 teaspoons cream cheese

3 tablespoons panko breadcrumbs

½ teaspoon salt

1 oz Parmesan, grated

½ teaspoon ground black pepper

1 teaspoon dried oregano

1 tablespoon sunflower oil

Directions:

1. Grind the fish fillet and combine it with cream cheese, panko breadcrumbs, salt, Parmesan, ground black pepper, and dried oregano.

2. Then make the small balls from the mixture and place them in the non-stick tray.

3. Sprinkle the balls with sunflower oil and bake in the preheated to 365F oven for 15 minutes. Flip the balls on another side after 10 minutes of cooking.

Nutrition:

- Calories 180,
- Fat 10.2g,
- Fiber 0.5g,
- Carbs 2.8g,
- Protein 19.9g

FISH CHILI WITH CHICKPEAS

Preparation Time: 10 minutes

Cooking time: 30 minutes

Serving:4

Ingredients:

1 red pepper, chopped

1 yellow onion, diced

1 teaspoon ground black pepper

1 teaspoon butter

1 jalapeno pepper, chopped

½ cup chickpeas

3 cups chicken stock

1 teaspoon salt

1 tablespoon tomato paste

1 teaspoon chili pepper

3 tablespoons fresh cilantro, chopped

8 oz cod, chopped

Directions:

1. Place butter, red pepper, onion, and ground black pepper in the saucepan.
2. Roast the vegetables for 5 minutes over medium heat.
3. Then add chopped jalapeno pepper, chickpeas, and chili pepper.
4. Mix up the mixture well and add chicken stock and tomato paste.
5. Stir until homogenous. Add cod.
6. Close the lid and cook chili for 20 minutes over medium heat.

Nutrition:

- Calories 187,
- Fat 2.3g,
- Fiber 8.8g,
- Carbs 21.3g,
- Protein 20.6g

CHILI MUSSELS

Preparation Time: 7 minutes

Cooking time: 10 minutes

Serving:4

Ingredients:

1-pound mussels

1 chili pepper, chopped

1 cup chicken stock

½ cup milk

1 teaspoon olive oil

1 teaspoon minced garlic

1 teaspoon ground coriander

½ teaspoon salt

1 cup fresh parsley, chopped

4 tablespoons lemon juice

Directions:

1. Pour milk into the saucepan.
2. Add chili pepper, chicken stock, olive oil, minced garlic, ground coriander, salt, and lemon juice.
3. Bring the liquid to a boil and add mussels.
4. Boil the mussel for 4 minutes or until they will open the shells.
5. Then add chopped parsley and mix up the meal well.
6. Remove it from the heat.

Nutrition:

- Calories 136,
- Fat 4.7g,
- Fiber 0.6g,
- Carbs 7.5g,
- Protein 15.3g

FRIED SCALLOPS IN HEAVY CREAM

Preparation Time: 10 minutes

Cooking time: 7 minutes

Serving:4

Ingredients:

½ cup heavy cream

1 teaspoon fresh rosemary

½ teaspoon dried cumin

½ teaspoon garlic, diced

8 oz bay scallops

1 teaspoon olive oil

½ teaspoon salt

¼ teaspoon chili flakes

Directions:

1. Preheat olive oil in the skillet until hot.
2. Then sprinkle scallops with salt, chili flakes, and dried cumin and place in the hot oil.

3. Add fresh rosemary and diced garlic.
4. Roast the scallops for 2 minutes from each side.
5. After this, add heavy cream and bring the mixture to a boil. Boil it for 1 minute.

Nutrition:
- Calories 114,
- Fat 7.3g,
- Fiber 0.2g,
- Carbs 2.2g,
- Protein 9.9g

LETTUCE SEAFOOD WRAPS

Preparation Time: 10 minutes

Cooking time: 0 minutes

Serving:6

Ingredients:

6 lettuce leaves

8 oz cod, canned

4 oz crab meat, canned

1 cucumber

2 tablespoons soy yogurt

½ teaspoon minced garlic

1 tablespoon fresh dill, chopped

¼ teaspoon tarragon

Directions:
1. Mash the cod and crab meat with the help of the fork.
2. Then add soy yogurt, minced garlic, fresh dill, and tarragon.
3. Grate the cucumber and add it to the seafood mixture. Mix up well.
4. Fill the lettuce leaves with the cooked mixture.

Nutrition:
- Calories 80,
- Fat 2.8g,

- Fiber 0.4g,
- Carbs 3.1g,
- Protein 10.5g

MANGO TILAPIA FILLETS

Preparation Time: 10 minutes

Cooking time: 15 minutes

Serving: 4

Ingredients:

¼ cup coconut flakes

5 oz mango, peeled

1/3 cup shallot, chopped

1 teaspoon ground turmeric

1 cup of water

1 bay leaf

12 oz tilapia fillets

1 chili pepper, chopped

1 tablespoon coconut oil

½ teaspoon salt

1 teaspoon paprika

Directions:

1. Blend coconut flakes, mango, shallot, ground turmeric, and water.
2. After this, melt coconut oil in the saucepan.
3. Sprinkle the tilapia fillets with salt and paprika.
4. Then place them in the hot coconut oil and roast for 1 minute from each side.
5. Add chili pepper, bay leaf, and blended mango mixture.
6. Close the lid and cook the fish for 10 minutes over medium heat.

Nutrition:

- Calories 153,
- Fat 6.1g,
- Fiber 1.5g,
- Carbs 9.3g,

- Protein 16.8g

Preparation Time: 15 minutes

Cooking time: 40 minutes

Serving:5

Ingredients:

5 Carrots, sliced

½ cup onion, chopped

½ cup almond milk

1 egg, beaten

3 tablespoon wheat flour, whole grain

1 cup shrimps, peeled

½ cup Mozzarella cheese, shredded

¼ cup Cheddar cheese, shredded

1 teaspoon olive oil

1 cup water, for cooking

Directions:

1. Pour water into the pan and bring it to a boil.
2. Add sliced carrots to the hot water and boil it for 3 minutes.
3. Then remove carrots from water.
4. Mix up together beaten egg, milk, chopped onion, flour, and Cheddar cheese.
5. Preheat the mixture until the cheese is melted.
6. Then place the carrots in the gratin mold in one layer.
7. Add the layer of shrimps.
8. Pour Cheddar cheese mixture over shrimps and top the gratin with Mozzarella cheese.
9. Cover the gratin with foil and secure the edges.
10. Bake gratin for 35 minutes at 355F.

Nutrition:

- Calories 205,
- Fat 5.3g,

- Fiber 3.5g,
- Carbs 26.2g,
- Protein 14.1g

GINGER SEABASS STIR-FRY

Preparation Time: 10 minutes

Cooking time: 10 minutes

Serving:4

Ingredients:

1 teaspoon fresh ginger, minced

10 oz seabass fillet (4 fillets)

1 tablespoon butter

1 teaspoon minced garlic

¼ teaspoon ground nutmeg

½ teaspoon salt

Directions:

1. Toss butter in the skillet and melt it.
2. Add minced garlic, ground nutmeg, salt, and fresh ginger.
3. Roast the mixture for 1 minute.
4. Then add seabass fillet.
5. Fry the fish for 3 minutes from each side.

Nutrition:

- Calories 205,
- Fat 13.5g,
- Fiber 0.8g,
- Carbs 0.6g,
- Protein 19.7g

HEARTY MEATBALLS

Preparation time: 10 minutes

Cooking Time:20minutes

Serving: 3

Ingredients:

Meatball:

1 tablespoon lemon juice

¼ teaspoon dry mustard

¾ teaspoon onion powder

1 teaspoon Italian seasoning

1 teaspoon poultry seasoning, unsalted

1 teaspoon black pepper

1 pound lean ground beef or turkey

¼ cup onion, finely chopped

1 teaspoon granulated sugar

1 teaspoon Tabasco sauce

Sauce:

1 teaspoon onion powder

2 teaspoons vinegar

2 teaspoons sugar

¼ cup of vegetable oil

2 tablespoons all-purpose flour

1 teaspoon Tabasco sauce

2-3 cups water

Directions:

1. Preheat an oven to 425°F. Grease a baking dish with some cooking spray.
2. In a mixing bowl, add all meatball ingredients. Combine to mix well with each other.
3. Prepare meatballs from it and bake in a baking dish for 20 minutes until evenly brown.
4. Take a medium saucepan or skillet, add oil. Heat over medium heat.
5. Add flour, vinegar, sugar, onion powder, mild sauce, and water; stir-cook until sauce thickens.
6. Serve meatballs with sauce on top.

Nutrition:

- Calories: 176
- Fat: 11g
- Phosphorus: 91mg
- Potassium: 152mg
- Sodium: 61mg
- Carbohydrates: 6g
- Protein: 14g

Preparation Time: 15 minutes

Cooking Time: 1 hour 52 minutes

Serving: 6

Ingredients:

1 (2-inch) piece fresh ginger, chopped

5-10 garlic cloves, chopped

1 teaspoon ground cumin

½ teaspoon ground turmeric

1 tablespoon hot paprika

1 tablespoon red pepper flakes

Salt, to taste

2 tablespoons cider vinegar

2-pounds pork shoulder, trimmed and cubed into 1½-inch size

2 cups domestic hot water, divided

1 (1-inch wide) ball tamarind pulp

¼ cup olive oil

1 teaspoon black mustard seeds, crushed

4 green cardamoms

5 whole cloves

1 (3-inch) cinnamon stick

1 cup onion, chopped finely

1 large red bell pepper, seeded and chopped

Directions:

1. In a food processor, add ginger, garlic, cumin, turmeric, paprika, red pepper flakes, salt, and cider vinegar and pulse till smooth.
2. Transfer the amalgamation into a large bowl.
3. Add pork and coat with mixture generously.
4. Keep aside, covered for around an hour at room temperature.
5. In a bowl, add 1 cup of warm water and tamarind and make aside till water becomes cool.
6. With the hands, crush the tamarind to extract the pulp.
7. Add remaining cup of hot water and mix till well combined.
8. Through a fine sieve, strain the tamarind juice inside a bowl.
9. In a sizable skillet, heat oil on medium-high heat.
10. Add mustard seeds, green cardamoms, cloves, and cinnamon stick and sauté for about 4 minutes.
11. Add onion and sauté for approximately 5 minutes.
12. Add pork and stir fry for approximately 6 minutes.
13. Stir in tamarind juice and convey with a boil.
14. Reduce the heat to medium-low and simmer for 1½ hours.
15. Stir in bell pepper and cook for about 7 minutes.

Nutrition:

- Calories: 435,
- Fat: 16g,
- Carbohydrates: 27g,
- Fiber: 3g,
- Protein: 39g

PORK CHILI

Preparation Time: 15 minutes

Cooking Time: 1 hour

Serving: 6

Ingredients:

2 tablespoons extra-virgin organic olive oil

2-pound ground pork

1 medium red bell pepper, seeded and chopped

1 medium onion, chopped

5 garlic cloves, chopped finely

1 (2-inch) part of hot pepper, minced

1 tablespoon ground cumin

1 teaspoon ground turmeric

3 tablespoon chili powder

½ teaspoon chipotle chili powder

Salt and freshly ground black pepper, to taste

1 cup chicken broth

1 (28-ounce) can fire-roasted crushed tomatoes

2 medium Bok choy heads, sliced

Directions:

1. In a sizable pan, heat oil on medium heat.
2. Add pork and stir fry for about 5 minutes.
3. Add bell pepper, onion, garlic, hot pepper, and spices and stir fry for approximately 5 minutes.
4. Add broth and tomatoes and convey with a boil.
5. Stir in Bok choy and cook, covered for approximately twenty minutes.
6. Uncover and cook approximately 20-half an hour.
7. Serve hot.

Nutrition:

- Calories: 402,
- Fat: 9g,
- Carbohydrates: 18g,
- Fiber: 6g,
- Protein: 32g

GROUND PORK WITH WATER CHESTNUTS

Preparation Time: fifteen minutes

Cooking Time: 12 minutes

Serving: 6

Ingredients:

1 tablespoon plus 1 teaspoon coconut oil

1 tablespoon fresh ginger, minced

1 bunch scallion (white and green parts separated), chopped

1-pound lean ground pork

Salt, to taste

1 tablespoon 5-spice powder

1 (18-ounce) can water chestnuts, drained and chopped

1 tablespoon organic honey

2 tablespoons fresh lime juice

Directions:

1. In a big heavy-bottomed skillet, heat oil on high heat.
2. Add ginger and scallion whites and sauté for approximately ½-1½ minutes.
3. Add pork and cook for approximately 4-5 minutes.
4. Drain the extra fat from the skillet.
5. Add salt and 5-spice powder and cook for approximately 2-3 minutes.
6. Add scallion greens and remaining ingredients and cook, stirring continuously for about 1-2 minutes.

Nutrition:

- Calories: 520,
- Fat: 30g,
- Carbohydrates: 37g,
- Fiber: 4g,
- Protein: 25g

GLAZED PORK CHOPS WITH PEACH

Preparation Time: 15 minutes

Cooking Time: 16 minutes

Serving: 6

Ingredients:

2 boneless pork chops

Salt and freshly ground black pepper, to taste

1 ripe yellow peach, peeled, pitted, chopped, and divided

1 tbsp organic olive oil

2 tablespoons shallot, minced

2 tablespoons garlic, minced

2 tablespoons fresh ginger, minced

1 tablespoon organic honey

1 tablespoon balsamic vinegar

1 tablespoon coconut aminos

¼ teaspoon red pepper flakes, crushed

¼ cup water

Directions:

1. Sprinkle the pork chops with salt and black pepper generously.
2. In a blender, add 1 / 2 of peach and pulse till puree forms.
3. Reserve remaining peach.
4. In a skillet, heat oil on medium heat.
5. Add shallots and sauté for approximately 1-2 minutes.
6. Add garlic and ginger and sauté for approximately 1 minute.
7. Add remaining ingredients and lower heat to medium-low.
8. Bring to your boil and simmer for approximately 4-5 minutes or till a sticky glaze forms.
9. Remove from heat and reserve 1/3 with the glaze and keep aside.
10. Coat the chops with the remaining glaze.
11. Heat a nonstick skillet on medium-high heat.
12. Add chops and sear for around 4 minutes from both sides.
13. Transfer the chops to a plate and coat with all the remaining glaze evenly.
14. Top with reserved chopped peach and serve.

Nutrition:

- Calories: 446,
- Fat: 20g,
- Carbohydrates: 26g,
- Fiber: 5g,

- Protein: 38g

PORK CHOPS IN CREAMY SAUCE

Preparation Time: 15 minutes

Cooking Time: 14 minutes

Serving: 6

Ingredients:

2 garlic cloves, chopped

1 small jalapeño pepper, chopped

¼ cup fresh cilantro leaves

1½ teaspoons ground turmeric, divided

1 tablespoon fish sauce

2 tablespoons fresh lime juice

1 (13½-ounce) can coconut milk

4 (½-inch thick) pork chops

Salt, to taste

1 tablespoon coconut oil

1 shallot, chopped finely

Directions:

1. In a blender, add garlic, jalapeño pepper, cilantro, 1 teaspoon of ground turmeric, fish sauce, lime juice, and coconut milk and pulse till smooth.
2. Sprinkle the pork with salt and remaining turmeric evenly.
3. In a skillet, melt butter on medium-high heat.
4. Add shallots and sauté for approximately 1 minute.
5. Add chops and cook for approximately 2 minutes per side.
6. Transfer the chops inside a bowl.
7. Add coconut mixture and convey to your boil.
8. Reduce heat to medium and simmer, stirring occasionally for approximately 5 minutes.
9. Stir in pork chops and cook for about 3-4 minutes.
10. Serve hot.

Nutrition:

- Calories: 437,
- Fat: 9g,
- Carbohydrates: 21g,
- Fiber: 4g,
- Protein: 38g

BAKED PORK & ASPARAGUS MEATBALLS

Preparation Time: 15 minutes

Cooking Time: fifteen minutes

Serving: 6

Ingredients:

1-pound lean ground pork

1 organic egg white, beaten

4 asparagus, stemmed and minced

1 tablespoon fresh parsley, minced

1 tablespoon fresh basil leaves, minced

1 tablespoon fresh mint leaves, minced

2 teaspoons fresh lemon zest, grated finely

1½ teaspoons fresh ginger, grated finely

Salt and freshly ground black pepper, to taste

Directions:

1. Preheat the oven to 425 degrees F. Arrange the rack inside the center of the oven.
2. Line a baking sheet with parchment paper.
3. In a sizable bowl, add all ingredients and mix till well combined.
4. Make small equal-sized balls from the mixture.
5. Arrange the balls onto a prepared baking sheet in a single layer.
6. Bake for approximately 12-15 minutes or till done completely.

Nutrition:

- Calories: 411,
- Fat: 19g,
- Carbohydrates: 27g,

- Fiber: 11g,
- Protein: 35g

Carrots, Kale, and Ground Beef Breakfast Bowl

Preparation Time: 10 minutes

Cooking Time: 20 minutes

Serving: 3

Ingredients:

¼ cup coconut milk

1 to 2 tbsp coconut shavings

¼ tsp ground cinnamon

¼ tsp ground ginger

½ tsp spicy curry

1 tsp garam masala

10 large carrots, cooked

5 kale leaves, chopped

Salt and pepper to taste

¼-lb lean grass-fed beef

½ of a small onion, diced

1 cup Shiitake mushrooms

Coconut oil

Directions:

1. In a skillet, heat a small amount of coconut oil over medium-high heat. Sauté the mushroom and onions. Add the salt and pepper. Continue cooking for three minutes.
2. Add the ground beef, curry, garam masala, cinnamon, and ginger. Continue to cook until the beef turns brown.
3. Add the chopped kale and cook until the leaves wilt.
4. Stir in the coconut milk and add the cooked carrots. Continue cooking until the carrots break down.
5. Transfer to a bowl and garnish with coconut shavings. Serve warm.

Nutrition:

- Calories 225,
- Total Fat 14g,
- Saturated Fat 3g,
- Total Carbs 17g,
- Net Carbs 13g,
- Protein 10g,
- Sugar: 6g,
- Fiber 4g,
- Sodium 43mg,
- Potassium 469mg

LIGHT BEEF SOUP

Preparation Time: 10 minutes

Cooking Time: 1 hour and 10 minutes

Serving: 8

Ingredients:

1 tablespoon olive oil

1 large onion, chopped

2 cloves of garlic, minced

2 stalks celery, sliced

1-pound beef chuck, bones removed and cut into cubes

salt and pepper to taste

2 carrots, peeled and diced

½ teaspoon dried thyme

2 cups beef broth

2 cups chicken broth

2 cups water

1 bay leaf

Directions:

1. Heat the oil in a pot and sauté the onion, garlic, and celery until fragrant.
2. Stir in the beef chuck and season with salt and pepper.

3. Add the rest of the ingredients.
4. Close the lid and bring to a boil.
5. Allow simmering for 60 minutes until the beef is soft.
6. Serve and enjoy.

Nutrition:
- Calories 117,
- Total Fat 5g,
- Saturated Fat 1g,
- Total Carbs 5g,
- Net Carbs 4g,
- Protein 13g,
- Sugar: 2g,
- Fiber 1g,
- Sodium 546mg,
- Potassium 409mg

CHICKEN DUMPLINGS

Preparation Time: 10 minutes

Cooking Time: 20 minutes

Serving: 3

Ingredients:

1 pack rice paper wrappers

Water for sealing and steaming

Oil, for greasing

Dipping sauce:

¼ cup guava sauce

⅛ cup lime juice, freshly squeezed

Filling:

2 drops sesame oil

1 pound ground chicken

½ tablespoon fresh ginger, grated

½ tablespoon low-sodium soy sauce

½ cup carrots, grated

¼ cup fresh chives, minced

Pinch of white pepper

Directions:

1. Combine dipping sauce ingredients in a small bowl. Set aside.

2. Place a small piece of parchment paper on the bottom of the bamboo steaming basket; lightly grease with oil. Half-fill steaming pot with water; set over high heat. Bring to a boil.

3. Meanwhile, mix filling ingredients in a bowl. Take 1 wonton wrapper; dampen edges with water. Place a teaspoon of filling in the middle. Fold wrapper over, pressing gently to remove air pockets; pinch/crimp edges to seal. Place 3 or 4 dumplings per basket, making sure wrappers don't touch. Repeat step for multiple, stackable bamboo baskets; put a lid on.

4. Steam dumplings for 8 to 10 minutes, covered. Turn off the heat. Cool before removing basket(s) from the steaming pot. Place bamboo steaming basket on a serving tray with a small amount of dipping sauce on the side. Serve.

Nutrition:

- Protein 24.66g (45%),
- Potassium (K) 774 mg (16%) and
- Sodium, Na 381 mg (25%)

PITA POCKETS WITH CRAB AND CUCUMBER SALAD

Preparation Time: 10 minutes

Cooking Time: 30 minutes

Serving: 3

Ingredients:

4 servings Crab and Cucumber Salad

For the Bread (Dry Ingredients)

1 ½ teaspoons xanthan gum

½ teaspoon of sea salt

1 cup rice flour, finely milled

¼ cup arrowroot powder

¼ cup potato starch

For the Bread (Wet ingredients)

1 tablespoon coconut oil

1 tablespoon psyllium husk powder

1 teaspoon dry active yeast

1 teaspoon palm sugar, crumbled

1 cup warm water

Directions:

1. To make the bread: combine palm sugar, warm water, and yeast in a small bowl; rest until yeast becomes frothy. Stir in oil and psyllium husk powder.

2. Place dry ingredients in a large mixing bowl. Make a well in the middle; pour in wet ingredients. Mix until the dough comes together; rest the dough for 45 minutes. Divide into 4 equal portions. On a lightly floured surface, shape dough into balls. Roll each into ⅛ inch-thick disks.

3. Preheat oven to 450°F or 230°C for at least 15 minutes before baking; line 2 baking sheets with parchment paper. Place 2 pieces of pita bread on each sheet, making sure there are spaces for bread to expand in. Bake for 5 minutes on 1 side; flip. Bake the other side for 2 minutes. Bread will bloat and expand. Cool the pita bread completely to room temperature before slicing in half. Using your fingers, gently pry "pockets" open.

4. Divide Crab and Cucumber Salad into 8 equal portions: stuff portions into pita pockets. Serve.

Nutrition:

*   Protein 2.44g (4%),
*   Potassium (K) 130 mg (3%) and
*   Sodium, Na 157 mg (10%),
*   Without added salt content of sodium is 11mg (1%)

Preparation Time: 10 minutes

Cooking Time: 30 minutes

Serving: 3

Ingredients:

5 pieces pita, see Pita Pockets with Crab and Cucumber Salad

For bread-making instructions, kept warm

1 lime, sliced into wedges

For the Duck and Marinade:

4 duck breasts

1 tablespoon coconut oil

1 teaspoon Chinese cooking wine

1 teaspoon low-sodium soy sauce

Pinch of five-spice powder

For the Fillings:

3 tablespoons hoisin sauce

1 cucumber, julienned

¼ cup chives, minced

Directions:

1. Combine duck and marinade ingredients in a shallow dish; turn duck meat so it sits skin side-up. Marinate in the fridge uncovered for up to 12 hours to dry out the skin. Lightly drain meat just before frying.

2. Set a nonstick skillet over medium heat. Fry duck meat, skin side down first until golden and crispy. Flip; fry the other side until well seared but not burned. Do the same for the sides. Transfer cooked pieces on a sheet of aluminum foil; seal and rest for 10 minutes to bring out the juices. Just before serving, thinly slice the meat.

3. To assemble: spread a small amount of hoisin sauce on each warmed pita bread. Divide cucumber, chives, and the desired amount of duck meat amongst each serving. Fold; repeat the step

for remaining ingredients. Serve with a wedge of lime. Squeeze lime juice over fillings just before eating.

Nutrition:

- Protein 16.91g (31%),
- Potassium (K) 270 mg (6%) and
- Sodium, Na 238 mg (16%),
- Without added salt sodium content is 165 mg (11%)

TERIYAKI CHICKEN STIR-FRY

Preparation Time: 10 minutes

Cooking Time: 20 minutes

Serving: 3

Ingredients:

3 tablespoons peanut oil

2 tablespoons teriyaki sauce

2 white onions, julienned

1 chicken breast fillet, julienned

1 cup green beans, roughly chopped

¾ cup low-sodium chicken stock

¼ cup water

¼ teaspoon black pepper

¼ pound bok choy, sliced into inch-thick slivers

For the Cornstarch Slurry:

1 tablespoon cornstarch

1 tablespoon water

Directions:

1. Dissolve cornstarch in water. Set aside.
2. Pour oil into nonstick wok set over medium heat; add in chicken. Stir-fry meat until no longer pink and lightly seared on all sides. Except for cornstarch slurry, add remaining ingredients into wok; stir-fry for 5 minutes.

3. Pour in cornstarch slurry; cook until sauce thickens. Turn off the heat. Taste; adjust seasoning if needed. Spoon equal portions on plates. Serve.

Nutrition:

- Protein 16.21g (30%),
- Potassium (K) 590 mg (13%) and
- Sodium, Na 562 mg (37%)

BEEF AND VEGETABLE EGG ROLLS

Preparation Time: 10 minutes

Cooking Time: 30 minutes

Serving: 3

Ingredients:

1 rice paper wrapper

Water for sealing

Oil for deep frying

For the Dipping Sauce

1 bird's eye chili, minced

¼ cup guava sauce

¼ teaspoon palm sugar, crumbled

¼ teaspoon grated garlic

¼ teaspoon lime juice, freshly squeezed

For the Filling

2 garlic cloves, minced

2 leeks, minced

1 large onion, minced

1 carrot, julienned

1 tablespoon coconut oil

1 tablespoon teriyaki sauce

½ cup jicama, julienned

¼ cup frozen peas, thawed

¼ pound lean ground beef

Pinch of sea salt

Pinch of black pepper

Directions:

1. Combine dipping sauce in a small bowl. Set aside.

2. Pour coconut oil into nonstick wok set over medium heat; sauté garlic, leek, and onion until limp and transparent. Add in remaining ingredients; stir. Put a lid on. Reduce heat to the lowest setting. Cook for 15 minutes, or until carrots are fork-tender. Turn off the heat. Taste; adjust seasoning if needed. Cool before rolling.

3. To prepare rolls: place 1 heaped tablespoon of filling into rice paper wrapper; roll tightly, tucking in edges and sealing with water. Set aside. Repeat step for remaining filling/wrapper.

4. Half-fill deep fryer with oil set at medium heat; wait for the oil to become slightly smoky before sliding in spring rolls. Cook until spring rolls turn golden brown, about 5 to 7 minutes. Remove cooked spring rolls from the fryer; drain well on a plate lined with paper towels. Place the recommended number of spring rolls on a plate; serve with dipping sauce on the side.

Nutrition:

- Protein 13.97g (26%),
- Potassium (K) 430 mg (9%) and
- Sodium, Na 442 mg (29%)

BEEF NOODLE SOUP

Preparation Time: 20 minutes

Cooking Time: 25 minutes

Serving: 4

Ingredients:

4 cups zucchini, spiral

1 cup carrots, spiral

1 cup jicama, spiral

2 pcs Beef Knorr Cubes

8 cups water

freshly ground pepper to taste

3 stalks green onions, chopped

¼ lb beef, thinly sliced

4 tbsp ground pork rinds (chicharron), divided

2 hardboiled eggs, halved

1 tsp salt

Directions:

1. In a pot, bring water to a boil. Add Knorr cubes and fish sauce.

2. With a strainer, dip into the boiling water the zucchini noodles and cook for 3 minutes. Remove from water, drain and arrange into 4 bowls. If needed, you can cook zucchini noodles in batches.

3. Next, cook the carrots in the boiling pot of water using a strainer still. Around 2-3 minutes, drain and arrange on top of the zucchini noodles.

4. Do the same with jicama, cook in the pot, drain and arrange equally into the bowls.

5. Do the same for the thinly sliced beef. Cook for 5-10 minutes in the boiling pot of soup, swirling the strainer occasionally to ensure uniform cooking for the beef. Arrange equally on the 4 bowls.

6. Sprinkle 1 tbsp of ground pork rinds on each bowl, topped by chopped green onions, ½ hardboiled egg, and freshly ground pepper.

7. Taste the boiling pot of soup and adjust to your taste. It should be slightly saltier than usual so that the noodles will absorb the excess salt once you pour it into the bowls. Add more fish sauce to make it salty or add water to make the pot less salty. Keep soup on a rolling boil before pouring 1-2 cups of soup on each bowl. Serve right away.

Nutrition:

- Calories 101,
- Total Fat 4g,
- Saturated Fat 1g,
- Total Carbs 7g,
- Net Carbs g,

- Protein 10g,
- Sugar: 3g,
- Fiber 3g,
- Sodium 1100mg,
- Potassium 353mg

Preparation Time: 10 minutes

Cooking Time: 25 minutes

Serving: 2

Ingredients:

2 tablespoons chopped green bell pepper

1/4 teaspoon Worcestershire sauce

1/4 teaspoon ground cumin

1/4 cup finely chopped onion

1/4 cup chile sauce

1/3 cup uncooked long-grain, rice

1/2-pound lean ground beef

1/2 teaspoon salt

1/2 teaspoon brown sugar

1/2 pinch ground black pepper

1/2 cup water

1/2 (14.5 ounces) can canned tomatoes

1 tablespoon chopped fresh cilantro

Directions:

1. Place a nonstick saucepan on medium fire and brown beef for 10 minutes while crumbling beef. Discard fat.
2. Stir in pepper, Worcestershire sauce, cumin, brown sugar, salt, chile sauce, rice, water, tomatoes, green bell pepper, and onion. Mix well and cook for 10 minutes until blended and a bit tender.
3. Transfer to an ovenproof casserole and press down firmly. Broil for 3 minutes until the top is lightly browned.
4. Serve and enjoy with chopped cilantro.

Nutrition:

- Calories 437,
- Total Fat 16g,
- Saturated Fat 2.5g,
- Total Carbs 38g,
- Net Carbs 30g,
- Protein 38g,
- Sugar: 12g,
- Fiber 8g,
- Sodium 1144mg,
- Potassium 1235mg

KEFTA STYLED BEEF PATTIES WITH CUCUMBER SALAD

Preparation Time: 10 minutes

Cooking Time: 10 minutes

Serving: 4

Ingredients:

2 pcs of 6-inch pita, quartered

½ tsp freshly ground black pepper

1 tbsp fresh lemon juice

½ cup plain soy yogurt, fat-free

2 cups thinly sliced English cucumber

½ tsp ground cinnamon

½ tsp salt

1 tsp ground cumin

2 tsp ground coriander

1 tbsp peeled and chopped ginger

¼ cup cilantro, fresh

¼ cup plus 2 tbsp fresh parsley, chopped and divided

1 lb. ground sirloin

Directions:

1. On medium-high fire, preheat a grill pan coated with cooking spray.

2. In a medium bowl, mix cinnamon, salt, cumin, coriander, ginger, cilantro, parsley, and beef. Then divide the mixture equally into four parts and shape each portion into a patty ½ inch thick.

3. Then place patties on the pan cooking each side for three minutes or until desired doneness is achieved.

4. In a separate bowl, toss together vinegar and cucumber.

5. In a small bowl, whisk together pepper, juice, 2 tbsp parsley, and yogurt.

6. Serve each patty on a plate with ½ cup cucumber mixture and 2 tbsp of the yogurt sauce.

Nutrition:
- Calories 306,
- Total Fat 13g,
- Saturated Fat 2g,
- Total Carbs 11g,
- Net Carbs 9g,
- Protein 34g,
- Sugar: 2g,
- Fiber 2g,
- Sodium 433mg,
- Potassium 507mg

BROILED CHICKEN THIGHS CHOPS

Preparation Time: 10 minutes

Cooking Time: 10 minutes

Serving: 4

Ingredients:

Cooking spray

8 pcs of chicken thighs, around 4 oz

¼ tsp black pepper

½ tsp salt

1 tbsp bottled minced garlic

2 tbsps lemon juice

1 tbsp dried oregano

Directions:

1. Preheat broiler.
2. In a big bowl or dish, combine the black pepper, salt, minced garlic, lemon juice, and oregano. Then rub it equally on all sides of the chicken thighs.
3. Then coat a broiler pan with the cooking spray before placing the chicken thighs on the pan and broiling until the desired doneness is reached or for five minutes per side.

Nutrition:

- Calories 332,
- Total Fat 16g,
- Saturated Fat 2.3g,
- Total Carbs 3g,
- Net Carbs 2.7g,
- Protein 46g,
- Sugar: 0.6g,
- Fiber 0.3g,
- Sodium 466mg,
- Potassium 780mg

MUSTARD CHOPS WITH PLUM-BASIL RELISH

Preparation Time: 20 minutes

Cooking Time: 12 minutes

Serving: 4

Ingredients:

1 tsp ground cardamom

2 tbsp olive oil

3 tbsp raspberry vinegar

¼ cup basil, finely shredded

1 shallot, diced small

¾ lb. fresh plum, stone removed, and fruit diced

½ cup mustard

Pepper and salt

4 pork chops

Directions:

1. Make sure that pork chops are defrosted well. Season with pepper and salt. Slather both sides of each pork chop with mustard. Preheat grill to medium-high fire.

2. In a medium bowl, mix cardamom, olive oil, vinegar, basil, shallot, and plums. Toss to combine and season with pepper and salt, mixing once again.

3. Grill chops for 5 to 6 minutes per side. As you flip, baste with mustard.

4. Serve pork chops with the plum-Basil relish and enjoy.

Nutrition:

- Calories 488,
- Total Fat 25g,
- Saturated Fat 3.5g,
- Total Carbs 22g,
- Net Carbs 19g,
- Protein 42g,
- Sugar: 18g,
- Fiber 3g,
- Sodium 478mg,
- Potassium 763mg

SIRLOIN ROLLS WITH ASPARAGUS & FENNEL

Preparation Time: 10 minutes

Cooking Time: 50 minutes

Serving: 4

Ingredients:

3 fennel fronds

1 tsp olive oil

½ fennel bulb cut into thick slices

2 cups asparagus, roughly chopped

Pepper and salt to taste

2 pieces of ½ lb. each sirloin steak

Filling Ingredients:

1 tsp oregano

1 tsp sage

1 tsp rosemary

2 garlic cloves

½ fennel bulb, roughly chopped

Directions:

1. Preheat oven to 375oF.
2. In a blender, puree all filling ingredients.
3. With a mallet, pound steaks until ½-inch thick. Divide into two the pureed filling ingredients and spread on each steak. Roll steak and secure ends with a toothpick.
4. In a large roasting pan, place fennel and asparagus. Season with pepper, salt, and olive oil. Toss well to coat. Arrange sprouts and fennel on the side of the pan.
5. Place steaks in the middle of the roasting pan and season with pepper and salt.
6. Roast for 35 to 40 minutes. Remove steak if the desired doneness is reached and let it rest as you continue to roast veggies for another 5 to 10 minutes.

Nutrition:

- Calories 342,
- Total Fat 21g,
- Saturated Fat 4g,
- Total Carbs 12g,
- Net Carbs 7.5g,
- Protein 28g,
- Sugar: 4.4g,
- Fiber 4.5g,
- Sodium 168mg,
- Potassium 952mg

Preparation Time: 10 minutes

Cooking Time: 20 minutes

Serving: 4

Ingredients:

1 tsp ground paprika

1 tsp ground cumin

1 tsp ground coriander

1 tsp sea salt

4 bone-in pork chops, around 1 – 1 ½ inches thick

Slaw Ingredients:

A pinch of salt

1 tsp lime juice

1 tsp lime zest

¼ tsp ground chipotle powder

1 lb. assorted firm stone fruit >>Uplums, and peaches preferably)

Directions:

1. Grease grate and preheat grill to medium-high fire.
2. In a small bowl, mix well paprika, coriander, cumin, and salt. Rub spice evenly on all sides of pork chops.
3. Grill pork chops per side for five minutes. Remove from grill, transfer to a plate and loosely tent with foil and let it stand for at least 10 minutes.
4. Meanwhile, slice the firm stone fruits into thin strips and place in a bowl.
5. Add salt, lime juice, lime zest, and chipotle powder into a bowl, and toss well to coat.
6. To serve, place one pork chop per plate and top with ¼ of the fruit slaw mixture.

Nutrition:

- Calories 426,
- Total Fat 18g,

- Saturated Fat 2g,
- Total Carbs 25g,
- Net Carbs 23g,
- Protein 41g,
- Sugar: 23g,
- Fiber 2g,
- Sodium 674mg,
- Potassium 725mg

BEEF STEW

Preparation Time: 10 minutes

Cooking Time: 180 minutes

Serving: 4

Ingredients:

Pepper and salt to taste

1 tbsp olive oil

1 tbsp fresh coriander, roughly chopped

1 tbsp honey, optional

1 tbsp Ras el Hanout

2 cups beef stock

½ cup golden raisins

1 cup dried figs, cut in half

2 cloves garlic, minced

1 onion, minced

1 lb. beef, trimmed of fat and cut into 2-inch cubes

Spice Mixture:

¼ tsp ground cloves

½ tsp anise seeds'1/2 tsp ground cayenne pepper

½ tsp ground black pepper

1 tsp ground turmeric

1 tsp ground nutmeg

1 tsp ground allspice

1 tsp ground cinnamon

2 tsp ground mace

2 tsp ground cardamom

2 tsp ground ginger

Directions:

1. Preheat oven to 300oF.
2. In a small bowl, add all Ras el Hanout ingredients and mix thoroughly. Just get what the ingredients need and store remaining in a tightly lidded spice jar.
3. On high fire, place a heavy-bottomed medium pot and heat olive oil. Once hot, brown beef pieces on each side for around 3 to 4 minutes.
4. Lower fire to medium-high and add remaining ingredients, except for the coriander.
5. Mix well. Season with pepper and salt to taste. Cover pot and bring to a boil.
6. Once boiling, turn off the fire, and pop the pot into the oven.
7. Bake uncovered for 2 to 2.5 hours or until meat is fork-tender.
8. Once the meat is tender, remove it from the oven.
9. To serve, sprinkle fresh coriander, and enjoy.

Nutrition:

- Calories 566,
- Total Fat 16g,
- Saturated Fat 2g,
- Total Carbs 85g,
- Net Carbs 75g,
- Protein 28g,
- Sugar: 60g,
- Fiber 10g,
- Sodium 606mg,
- Potassium 1243mg

Chapter 5

Desserts

STRAWBERRY WHIPPED CREAM CAKE

Preparation Time: 10 minutes

Cooking Time: 20 minutes

Serving: 3

Ingredients:

1-pint whipping cream

2 tbsp. gelatin

1/2 glass cold water

1 glass boiling water

3 tbsp. lemon juice

1 grapefruit glass juice

1 tsp. sugar

3/4 cup sliced strawberries

1 large angel food cake or light sponge cake

Directions:

1. Put the gelatin in cold water then add hot water and blend. Add grapefruit and lemon juice, also add some sugar and go on blending.

2. Refrigerate and leave it there until you see it is starting to gel.

3. Whip half portion of cream and add it to the mixture along with strawberries, put wax paper in the bowl, and cut the cake into small pieces.

4. In between the pieces, add the whipped cream and put everything in the fridge for one night.

5. When you take out the cake, add some whipped cream on top and decorate with some more fruit. Serve and enjoy!

Nutrition:

- Calories: 355
- Protein: 4 g
- Sodium: 275 mg
- Potassium: 145 mg
- Phosphorus: 145 mg

SWEET CRACKER PIE CRUST

Preparation Time: 10 minutes

Cooking Time: 30 minutes

Serving: 3

Ingredients:

1 bowl gelatin cracker crumbs

1/4 small cup sugar

Unsalted butter

Directions:

1. Mix sweet cracker crumbs, butter, and sugar.

2. Put in the oven preheat at 375°F.

3. Bake for 7 minutes putting it in a greased pie.

4. Let the pie cool before adding any kind of filling. Serve and enjoy!

Nutrition:

- Calories: 205
- Protein: 2 g
- Sodium: 208 mg
- Potassium: 67 mg
- Phosphorus: 22 mg

APPLE OATMEAL CRUNCHY

Preparation Time: 10 minutes

Cooking Time: 40 minutes

Serving: 3

Ingredients:

5 green apples

1 bowl oatmeal

A small cup of brown sugar

1/2 cup flour

1 tsp. cinnamon

1/2 bowl butter

Directions:

1. Prepare apples by cutting them into tiny slices and preheat the oven at 350°F.
2. In a cup mix oatmeal, flour, cinnamon, and brown sugar.
3. Put butter in the batter and place sliced apple in a baking pan (9" x 13").
4. Spread oatmeal mixture over the apples and bake for 35 minutes. Serve and enjoy!

Nutrition:

- Calories: 295
- Protein: 3 g
- Sodium: 95 mg
- Potassium: 190 mg
- Phosphorus: 73 mg

Preparation time: 10 minutes

Cooking time: 20 minutes

Serving: 2

Ingredients:

2 cups blueberries

6 cups sourdough bread cubes

1/2 tsp. ground cinnamon

2 tsp. vanilla

3 eggs

1/2 cup honey

3 cups unsweetened rice milk

Directions:

1. Warm your oven to 350 F.
2. Add cinnamon, vanilla, eggs, honey, and rice milk to a large bowl until well-blended.
3. Add in the bread cubes. Allow the bread to soak for 30 minutes.
4. Add in the blueberries. Stir well to combine. Pour into a 13 x 9 baking dish.
5. Bake for 35 minutes. Check to see if it's done by poking it in the center with a toothpick and it comes out clean. Serve and enjoy!

Nutrition:

- Calories: 382
- Protein: 11 g
- Sodium: 378 mg
- Potassium: 170 mg
- Phosphorus: 120 mg

ALMOND COOKIES

Preparation time: 10 minutes

Cooking time: 35 minutes

Serving: 24

Ingredients:

1 tsp cream of tartar

2 egg whites or 4 tbsp pasteurized egg whites

½ tsp vanilla extract

½ tsp almond extract

½ cup white sugar

Directions:

1. Preheat oven to 300°F.
2. Beat egg whites with cream of tartar.
3. Add remaining ingredients.
4. Beat until firm peaks are formed.
5. Push one teaspoon full of meringue onto a parchment-lined cookie sheet with the back of the other spoon.
6. Bake for approximately 25 minutes or until meringues is crisp.

Nutrition:

- Protein - 0.6g
- Carbohydrates - 9g
- Fat - 0g
- Calories - 37.9

SEMOLINA PUDDING

Preparation Time: 15 minutes

Cooking time: 7 minutes

Serving:3

Ingredients:

½ cup organic almond milk

½ cup coconut milk

1/3 cup semolina

1 tablespoon butter

¼ teaspoon cornstarch

½ teaspoon almond extract

Directions:

1. Pour almond milk and coconut milk into the saucepan.

2. Bring it to boil and add semolina and cornstarch.
3. Mix up the ingredients until homogenous and simmer them for 1 minute.
4. After this, add almond extract and butter. Stir well and close the lid.
5. Remove the pudding from the heat and leave for 10 minutes.
6. Then mix it up again and transfer in the serving ramekins.

Nutrition:
- Calories 201,
- Fat 7.9g,
- Fiber 1.1g,
- Carbs 25.7g,
- Protein 5.8 g

WATERMELON JELLY

Preparation Time: 30 minutes

Cooking time: 5 minutes

Serving:2

Ingredients:

8 oz watermelon

1 tablespoon gelatin powder

Directions:
1. Make the juice from the watermelon with the help of the fruit juicer.
2. Combine 5 tablespoons of watermelon juice and 1 tablespoon of gelatin powder. Stir it and leave for 5 minutes.
3. Then preheat the watermelon juice until warm, add gelatin mixture, and heat it over medium heat until gelatin is dissolved.
4. Then remove the liquid from the heat and pout it in the silicone molds.
5. Freeze the jelly for 30 minutes in the freezer or 4 hours in the fridge.

Nutrition:

- Calories 46,
- Fat 0.2g,
- Fiber 0.4g,
- Carbs 8.5g,
- Protein 3.7g

Preparation Time: 20 minutes

Cooking time: 725 minutes

Serving: 6

Ingredients:

½ cup soy yogurt

½ teaspoon baking powder

2 tablespoons Erythritol

1 teaspoon almond extract

½ teaspoon ground clove

½ teaspoon orange zest, grated

3 tablespoons walnuts, chopped

1 cup wheat flour

1 teaspoon butter, softened

1 tablespoon honey

3 tablespoons water

Directions:

1. In the mixing bowl mix up together soy yogurt, baking powder, Erythritol, almond extract, ground cloves orange zest, flour, and butter.

2. Knead the non-sticky dough. Add olive oil if the dough is very sticky and knead it well.

3. Then make the log from the dough and cut it into small pieces.

4. Roll every piece of dough into the balls and transfer it in the lined with baking paper tray.

5. Press the balls gently and bake for 25 minutes at 350F.

6. Meanwhile, heat up together honey and water. Simmer the liquid for 1 minute and remove from the heat.
7. When the cookies are cooked, remove them from the oven and let them cool for 5 minutes.
8. Then pour the cookies with sweet honey water and sprinkle with walnuts.
9. Cool the cookies.

Nutrition:
- Calories 134,
- Fat 3.4g,
- Fiber 0.9g,
- Carbs 26.1g,
- Protein 4.3g

BAKED FIGS WITH HONEY

Preparation Time: 10 minutes

Cooking time: 15 minutes

Serving:4

Ingredients:

4 figs

4 teaspoons honey

1 oz Blue cheese, chopped

Directions:
1. Make the cross cuts in the figs and fill them with chopped Blue cheese.
2. Then sprinkle the figs with honey and wrap them in the foil.
3. Bake the figs for 15 minutes at 355F.
4. Remove the figs from the foil and transfer them to the serving plates.

Nutrition:
- Calories 94,
- Fat 2.2g,
- Fiber 1.9g,

- Carbs 18.1g,
- Protein 2.2 g

CREAM STRAWBERRY PIES

Preparation Time: 20 minutes

Cooking time: 15 minutes

Serving:6

Ingredients:

1 cup strawberries

7 oz puff pastry

3 teaspoons butter, softened

3 teaspoons Erythritol

¼ teaspoon ground nutmeg

4 teaspoons cream

Directions:

1. Roll up the puff pastry and cut it into 6 squares.
2. Slice the strawberries.
3. Grease every puff pastry square with butter and then place the sliced strawberries on it.
4. Sprinkle every strawberry square with cream, ground nutmeg, and Erythritol.
5. Secure the edges of every puff pastry square in the shape of a pie.
6. Line the baking tray with baking paper.
7. Transfer the pies to the tray and place the tray in the oven.
8. Bake the pies for 15 minutes at 375F.

Nutrition:

- Calories 209,
- Fat 14.8g,
- Fiber 1g,
- Carbs 19.4g,
- Protein 2.6 g

Preparation Time: 7 minutes

Cooking time: 5 minutes

Serving:4

Ingredients:

10 oz fresh pineapple

½ teaspoon ground ginger

1 tablespoon almond butter, softened

Directions:

1. Slice the pineapple into the serving pieces and brush with almond butter.
2. After this, sprinkle every pineapple piece with ground ginger.
3. Preheat the grill to 400F.
4. Grill the pineapple for 2 minutes from each side.
5. The cooked fruit should have a light brown surface on both sides.

Nutrition:

- Calories 61,
- Fat 2.4g,
- Fiber 1.4g,
- Carbs 10.2g,
- Protein 1.3g

Preparation Time: 35 minutes

Cooking time: 1 minute

Serving:6

Ingredients:

3 tablespoons coconut butter

½ cup coconut flakes

1 egg, beaten

1 tablespoon cocoa powder

3 oz low sodium crackers, crushed

2 tablespoons Erythritol

3 tablespoons butter

1 teaspoon mint extract

1 teaspoon stevia powder

1 teaspoon of cocoa powder

1 tablespoon almond butter, melted

Directions:

1. Churn together coconut butter, coconut flakes, and 1 tablespoon of cocoa powder.
2. Then microwave the mixture for 1 minute or until it is melted.
3. Chill the liquid for 1 minute and fast add egg. Whisk it until homogenous and smooth.
4. Stir the liquid in the crackers and transfer it to the mold. Flatten it well with the help of the spoon.
5. After this, blend Erythritol, butter, mint extract, and stevia powder.
6. When the mixture is fluffy, place it over the crackers layer.
7. Then mix up together 1 teaspoon of cocoa powder and almond butter.
8. Sprinkle the cooked mixture with cocoa liquid and flatten it.
9. Refrigerate the dessert for 30 minutes.
10. Then cut it into the bars.

Nutrition:

- Calories 213,
- Fat 16.3g,
- Fiber 2.9g,
- Carbs 20g,
- Protein 3.5 g

HUMMINGBIRD CAKE

Preparation Time: 20 minutes

Cooking time: 30 minutes

Serving: 10

Ingredients:

1 cup of rice flour

1 cup coconut flour

½ cup wheat flour

½ cup Erythritol

½ teaspoon baking powder

¾ teaspoon salt

1/3 teaspoon ground cinnamon

½ cup olive oil

2 eggs, beaten

3 oz pineapple, chopped

1 pear, chopped

3 tablespoons Macadamia nuts, chopped

6 tablespoons cream cheese

Directions:

1. In the mixing bowl combine 9 first ingredients from the list above.
2. When the mixture is smooth and adds pineapple and pear.
3. Add Macadamia nuts and mix up the dough well.
4. Put the dough into the baking pans and bake for 30 minutes at 355F.
5. Then remove the cooked cakes from the oven and chill well.
6. Spread every cake with cream cheese and form them into 1 big cake.

Nutrition:

- Calories 278,
- Fat 16g,
- Fiber 6g,
- Carbs 41.9g,
- Protein 5.5g

Preparation Time: 8 minutes

Cooking time: 30 minutes

Serving:6

Ingredients:

2 cups coconut cream, chipped

6 teaspoons honey

2 mangoes, chopped

Directions:

1. Blend honey and mango.
2. When the mixture is smooth, combine it with whipped cream and stir carefully.
3. Put the mango-cream mixture in the serving glasses and refrigerate for 30 minutes.

Nutrition:

- Calories 272,
- Fat 19.5g,
- Fiber 3.6g,
- Carbs 27g,
- Protein 2.8g

BLUEBERRY AND APPLE CRISP

Preparation time: 10 minutes

Cooking time: 25 minutes

Serving: 8

Ingredients:

4 tp cornstarch

½ cup brown sugar

2 cups grated or chopped apples

4 cups of fresh or frozen blueberries (not thawed)

1 tbsp lemon juice

1 tbsp margarine, melted

¼ cup brown sugar

1¼ cups quick-cooking rolled oats

6 tbsp nonhydrogenated margarine, melted

¼ cup unbleached all-purpose flour

Directions:

1. Preheat the oven to 350°F.
2. Combine the dry ingredients in the bowl.
3. Add butter. Stir until moistened. Set aside.
4. Combine cornstarch and brown sugar.
5. Add lemon juice and fruits. Toss.
6. Top with the crisp mixture.
7. Bake for 1 hour until golden brown.
8. Serve warm or cold.

Nutrition:

- Protein - 3.3g
- Carbohydrates - 52g
- Fat - 12g
- Calories - 318

BERRY FRUIT SALAD WITH YOGURT

Preparation time: 10 minutes

Cooking time: 10 minutes

Serving: 8

Ingredients:

¼ cup honey

2 cups coconut yogurt

1 tbsp lemon juice

1 cup blackberries

1 cup red cherries, pitted and halved

1 cup blueberries

1 cup raspberries

2 tbsp honey

Directions:

1. Combine the berries with the honey in a bowl.
2. Mix the yogurt, lemon juice, and honey in a separate bowl.
3. Place yogurt cream into the center of each glass.
4. Garnish with the berry fruit salad.

Nutrition:

- Protein - 3.7g
- Carbohydrates – 27g
- Fat - 0.4g
- Calories - 117

AMBROSIA

Preparation time: 1 hour

Cooking time: 25 minutes

Serving: 12

Ingredients:

½ cup powdered sugar

1 cup sour cream

15 ounces canned pineapple chunks

½ tsp vanilla extract

1-½ cup maraschino cherries

15 ounces canned sliced peaches

3 cups miniature marshmallows

Directions:

1. Mix vanilla, powdered sugar, and sour cream in a bowl.
2. Drain cherries, peaches, and pineapple.
3. Add marshmallows and fruits to sour cream mixture.
4. Let chill for an hour.
5. Serve.

Nutrition:

- Protein - 1 g
- Carbohydrates - 36 g
- Fat - 4 g

- Calories - 176

APPLE BARS

Preparation time: 15 minutes

Cooking time: 50 minutes

Serving: 18

Ingredients:

¾ cup unsalted butter

2 medium apples

1 cup sour cream

1 cup granulated sugar

1 tsp baking soda

1 tsp vanilla extract

2 cups all-purpose flour

½ tsp salt

1 tsp cinnamon

½ cup brown sugar

1 cup powdered sugar

2 tbsp soy milk

Directions:

1. Preheat the oven to 350° F.
2. Chop and peel the apples.
3. Cream together ½ cup the granulated sugar and the butter.
4. Add flour, salt, baking soda, vanilla, and sour cream. Stir to mix.
5. Add apples.
6. Pour the batter into a greased 9" x 13" baking pan.
7. Put cinnamon, brown sugar, and 2 tablespoons of softened butter in a small bowl.
8. Bake for 40 minutes.
9. Let it cool and cut in 18 bars.

Nutrition:

- Protein - 2 g
- Carbohydrates - 35 g

- Fat - 11 g
- Calories - 246

BERRY ICE CREAM

Preparation time: 15 minutes

Cooking time: 50 minutes

Serving: 18

Ingredients:

6 ice cream cones

1 cup whipped topping

1 cup fresh blueberries

4 oz. cream cheese

1/4 cup blueberry jam

Directions:

1. Put the cream cheese in a large cup and beat it with a mixer until it is fluffy.
2. Mix with fruit and jam and whipped topping.
3. Put the mixture on the small ice cream cones and refrigerate them in the freezer for 1 hour or more until they are ready to serve. Enjoy!

Nutrition:

- Calories: 175
- Protein: 3 g
- Sodium: 95 mg
- Potassium: 80 mg
- Phosphorus: 40 mg

VANILLA CUSTARD

Preparation time: 5 minutes

Cooking time: 30 minutes

Serving: 3

Ingredients:

Artificial sweetener

1 large vegan egg

1/8 tsp. vanilla

1/8 tsp. nutmeg

½ cup low-fat milk

2 tbsps. stevia

Directions:

1. Scald the milk then let it cool slightly.
2. Break the egg into a small bowl and beat it with the nutmeg
3. Add the scalded milk, the vanilla, and the sweetener to taste; then mix very well
4. Place the bowl in a baking pan filled with ½ deep of water and bake for about 30 minutes at a temperature of about 325° F
5. Serve and enjoy your custard!

Nutrition:

- Calories 167.3,
- Fat 9g,
- Carbs 11g,
- Potassium (K) 249mg,
- Sodium (Na) 124mg,
- Phosphorous 205g,
- Protein 10g

ALMOND COOKIES

Preparation time: 7 minutes

Cooking time: 10 minutes

Serving: 10

Ingredients:

1 tsp. almond extract

1 cup stevia

1 tsp. baking soda

1 vegan egg

1 cup softened margarine

3 cups white flour

Directions:

1. Cream the margarine in a bowl; then add the stevia to it and beat very well

2. Sift your dry ingredients and add it to the creamed mixture

3. Add in the almond extract and mix very well.

4. Roll the dough into balls of about ¾ inches in diameter.

5. Make a small hole in each of the cookies and bake for about 12 minutes at a temperature of 400° F

6. Let the cookies cool for about 10 minutes

7. Serve and enjoy your dessert!

Nutrition:

- Calories 88,
- Fat 5g,
- Carbs 8g,
- Potassium (K) 28mg,
- Sodium (Na) 99mg,
- Phosphorous 30g,
- Protein 2.3g

RAISINS COOKIES

Preparation time: 7 minutes

Cooking time: 10 minutes

Serving: 10

Ingredients:

½ cup raisins

½ tsp. baking soda

½ tsp. vanilla

¼ tsp. salt

1 beaten vegan egg

1 cup flour

½ cup margarine

4 tsps. stevia

Directions:

1. Sift your dry ingredients all together
2. Cream the margarine; the stevia, the vanilla, and the egg and whisk very well
3. Add flour mixture and beat again
4. Stir in the raisins; then drop teaspoonfuls of the mixture over a greased baking sheet
5. Bake your cookies for about 10 minutes at a temperature of 375° F
6. Let your cookies cool for 5 minutes
7. Serve and enjoy your raisins cookies!

Nutrition:

*   Calories 106.2,
*   Fat 7g,
*   Carbs 8.9g,
*   Potassium (K) 28mg,
*   Sodium (Na) 98mg,
*   Phosphorous 19g,
*   Protein 1.5g

FRUIT COMPOTE

Preparation time:5 minutes

Cooking time:30 minutes

Serving:3

Ingredients:

28 oz. pineapple chunks

28 oz. pear slices

For the filling:

¼ cup melted margarine

2 cups crushed almond flakes

Directions:

1. Wash and drain your fruits very well; then grease a baking pan with cooking spray

2. Cut your fruits into slices; then arrange the fruit slices in the bottom of your baking pan
3. Crush the Grease a 9 x 13-inch pan and layer fruit, ending with pie filling.
4. Crush the almond flakes; then mix it with the margarine and sprinkle it over the fruits
5. Bake your pie for about 30 minutes at a temperature of 350°F
6. Serve and enjoy your dessert!

Nutrition:
- Calories 135.2,
- Fats 10g,
- Carbs 8.5g,
- Potassium (K) 286mg,
- Sodium (Na) 115mg,
- Phosphorous 32g,
- Protein 2.5g

Puffed Cereal Bars

Preparation time:5 minutes
Cooking time:10 minutes
Serving:10
Ingredients:
8 cups puffed rice cereal
1 ½ cups stevia
1/3 cup margarine
1 tsp. maple extract
Directions:
1. In a large saucepan and over medium-high heat, melt the margarine; then stir in the stevia, the maple extract and let boil for about 7 to 10 minutes
2. Stir in the puffed rice cereal; then let the mixture cool for about 5 minutes

3. Press the mixture into a greased baking pan and let chill for about 15 minutes
4. Cut into about 20 bars
5. Serve and enjoy your dessert!

Nutrition:

- Calories 111,
- Fat 7.9g,
- Carbs 6.4g,
- Potassium (K) 10mg,
- Sodium (Na) 26mg,
- Phosphorous 15g,
- Protein 3g

BUTTERMILK CAKE

Preparation time:5 minutes

Cooking time:10 minutes

Serving:10

Ingredients:

1 buttermilk cup

1 deep dish of 9-inch pie crust

2 tsp. lemon juice

2 eggs

1/4 buttercup

1 tsp. almond extract

1 tsp. vanilla extract

1/2 cup sugar

4 tsp. flour

Directions:

1. In a large bowl mix together eggs, softened butter (pre-cooked and softened at 375°F), buttermilk, almond and vanilla extract, sugar, and flour.
2. Put the mixture in a dish for pie crust and bake it for one hour.
3. Leave it aside to cool and then serve it in slices. Enjoy!

Nutrition:

- Calories: 373
- Protein: 4 g
- Sodium: 145 mg
- Potassium: 90 mg
- Phosphorus: 65 mg

CARAMEL PIE WITH APPLES

Preparation time:5 minutes

Cooking time:30 minutes

Serving:4

Ingredients:

3 bug apples

8 oz. frozen dessert topping

2 caramel nut blast gold bars

Directions:

1. Cut apples into small pieces and also cut caramel bars into small pieces.
2. Prepare whipped cream out of the fridge and mix it with caramel bar and apple pieces in a large bowl.
3. Cool it for one hour before eating it. Serve and enjoy!

Nutrition:

- Calories: 200
- Protein: 5 g
- Sodium: 45 mg
- Potassium: 115 mg
- Phosphorus: 45 mg

RASPBERRY PIE

Preparation time:5 minutes

Cooking time:30 minutes

Serving:4

Ingredients:

2 eggs

1 small cup granulated sugar

Some sour cream

1 tsp. vanilla

1/2 cup unsalted butter

2 tsp. white flour

1 tsp. baking powder

1 tsp. baking soda

20 oz. raspberry pie filling or 10 raspberry to be beaten and put in the cake

Directions:

1. Use a mixer and make soft all together softened butter, sugar, eggs, vanilla, and sour cream.
2. Preheat the oven at 350°F (or 200°C) in another bowl put together flour, baking powder, and baking soda.
3. Mix all together both dry and soft ingredients and pour the batter into a cooking dish for the oven. You can disperse raspberry pie filling or/and the cherries on the batter.
4. Bake in the oven for 40 - 45 minutes. Serve and enjoy!

Nutrition:

- Calories: 20
- Protein: 3 g
- Sodium: 110 mg
- Potassium: 70 mg
- Phosphorus: 70 mg

CRANBERRY DESSERT

Preparation time:5 minutes

Cooking time:30 minutes

Serving:4

Ingredients:

Cherry gelatin mix

Boiling water

12 oz. cranberries

1/2 glass sugar

12 oz. canned jelly cranberry sauce

12 oz. free whipped topping

Directions:

1. Put the gelatin mix in the boiled water and set aside, letting it cool down. Put sugar in another boiling water. Then add the cranberries and boil for 5 minutes.

2. When hot, remove the cranberries and add jellied cranberry sauce. Blend all together and break the jelly sauce into little chunks.

3. Add cool gelatin and whipped topping.

4. Distribute topping throughout and removing it from the heat, cool it for one hour.

5. Serve it cold. Enjoy!

Nutrition:

- Calories: 195
- Protein: 1 g
- Sodium: 35 mg
- Potassium: 30 mg
- Phosphorus: 10 mg

Chapter 6

Juices and Smoothies

APPLE AND BEET JUICE MIX

Preparation time: 5 minutes

Cooking time: 5 minutes

Serving: 2

Ingredients:

½ medium beet

½ medium apple

1 celery stalk

1 medium fresh carrot

¼ cup parsley

Directions:

1. Juice all ingredients.

2. Pour the mixture into 2 glasses.

Nutrition:
- Protein - 1 g
- Carbohydrates - 13 g
- Fat - 0 g
- Calories - 53

Assorted Fresh Fruit Juice

Preparation time: 5 minutes

Cooking time: 0 minutes

Serving:1

Ingredients:

1 roughly chopped apple

¼ cup halved frozen grapes

1 cup ice shavings

Directions:
1. Add all ingredients into the blender.
2. Process until smooth.
3. Pour equal portions into glasses. Serve immediately.

Nutrition:
- Calories 112
- Protein 1.16g
- Potassium (K) 367 mg
- Sodium (Na) 3 mg
- Fat 0.5g
- Carbs 25.8g
- Phosphorus 17.4mg

Berry Mint Water

Preparation time: 3 minutes

Cooking time: 5 minutes

Serving: 2

Ingredients:

3 mint springs

1/2 cup blackberries

1/2 cup strawberries

8 cups water

Directions:

1. Mix everything in a glass pitcher and allow to chill for an hour before serving.
2. Serve and enjoy!

Nutrition:

- Calories: 7
- Protein: 0 g
- Sodium: 0 mg
- Potassium: 28 mg
- Phosphorus: 4 mg

CINNAMON APPLE WATER

Preparation time: 5 minutes

Cooking time: 5 minutes

Serving: 10

Ingredients:

1 medium apple, thinly sliced

10 cups water

2 tsp ground cinnamon

2 cinnamon sticks

Directions:

Put all ingredients in a pitcher.

Refrigerate overnight.

Serve.

Nutrition:

- Protein - 0 g
- Carbohydrates - 1 g
- Fat - 0 g

- Calories - 4

FENNEL DIGESTIVE COOLER

Preparation time: 3 minutes

Cooking time: 5 minutes

Serving: 2

Ingredients:

1 tsp. honey

1/4 tsp. ground cloves

1/4 cup ground fennel seeds

2 cups unsweetened rice milk

Directions:

1. Blend everything in a blender and allow to rest for 30 minutes.
2. Pour through a wire sieve lined with cheesecloth.
3. Pour into 2 glasses. Serve and enjoy!

Nutrition:

- Calories: 163
- Protein: 3 g
- Sodium: 141 mg
- Potassium: 205 mg
- Phosphorus: 57 mg

TROPICAL JUICE

Preparation time: 3 minutes

Cooking time: 0 minutes

Serving: 2

Ingredients:

1 cup water

1/2 cup low fat coconut milk

1/2 cup chunked pineapple

Directions:

1. Combine everything in a blender.

2. Blend until smooth.

3. Pour into 2 glasses. Serve and enjoy!

Nutrition:

- Calories: 55
- Protein: 7 g
- Sodium: 111 mg
- Potassium: 129 mg
- Phosphorus: 11 mg

GREEN TEA WITH ARUGULA LEAVES, LIME, AND KALE LEAVES

Preparation time: 5 minutes

Cooking time: 5 minutes

Serving: 2

Ingredients:

1 quart (4 cups) filtered or spring water

4 tea bags green tea

2 pieces, large lime, sliced into bite-sized wedges, remove pips

¼ cup, tightly packed arugula leaves, rinsed well, drained

¼ cup, tightly packed kale leaves, rinsed well, drained

Directions:

1. Place all ingredients into a large pitcher. Mix while gently bruising lime wedges and leaves. Set aside for at least 4 to 6 hours in the fridge.

2. Strain out leaves and tea bags. Pour green tea with lime wedges. Always serve chilled.

Nutrition:

- Protein 0.47g (1%),
- Potassium (K) 60 mg (1%) and
- Sodium, Na 12 mg (1%)

Preparation time: 5 minutes

Cooking time: 5 minutes

Serving: 2

Ingredients:

1 quart (4 cups) filtered or spring water

4 tea bags white tea

2 cups watermelon flesh, deseeded, cut into large cubes

2 pieces, small apples, cored, diced into bite-sized pieces

1 sprig, large mint

Directions:

1. Place all ingredients into a large pitcher. Mix while gently bruising fruits and mint.

2. Set aside for at least 4 to 6 hours in the fridge. Strain out mint sprig and tea bags. Pour tea with fruits. Always serve chilled.

Nutrition:

- Protein 0.69g (1%),
- Potassium (K) 168 mg (4%) and
- Sodium, Na 4 mg (0%)

WHITE TEA WITH PEACHES AND MINT

Preparation time: 5 minutes

Cooking time: 5 minutes

Serving: 2

Ingredients:

1 quart (4 cups) filtered or spring water

4 tea bags white tea

2 pieces, large ripe peaches, pitted, sliced into bite-sized wedges

1 sprig, large mint, rinsed well, drained

Directions:

1. Place all ingredients into a large pitcher. Mix while gently bruising peaches and mint. Set aside for at least 4 to 6 hours in the fridge.

2. Strain out mint and tea bags. Pour tea with peach wedges. Always serve chilled.

Nutrition:
- Protein 0.88g (2%),
- Potassium (K) 178 mg (4%) and
- Sodium, Na 3 mg (0%)

WHITE TEA WITH SPICED APPLES

Preparation time: 5 minutes

Cooking time: 5 minutes

Serving: 2

Ingredients:

1 quart (4 cups) filtered or spring water

4 tea bags white tea

2 pieces, small apples, cored, diced into bite-sized pieces

1 piece, 2-inch long cinnamon stick

Directions:
1. Place all ingredients into a large pitcher. Mix while gently bruising fruits.
2. Set aside for at least 4 to 6 hours in the fridge. Strain out the cinnamon stick and tea bags. Pour tea with fruits. Always serve chilled.

Nutrition:
- Protein 0.71g (1%),
- Potassium (K) 203 mg (4%) and
- Sodium, Na 6 mg (0%)

PLUM, BLUEBERRY AND PEACH INFUSION

Preparation time: 5 minutes

Cooking time: 5 minutes

Serving: 2

Ingredients:

1 quart (4 cups) filtered or spring water

3 piece, large plum, peeled, pitted, cubed

1 piece, large peach, peeled, pitted, cubed

15 blueberries, washed

Directions:

1. Place all ingredients into a large pitcher. Mix while gently bruising fruits.

2. Set aside for at least an hour in the fridge. Pour drink. Consume liquid and fruits. Serve.

Nutrition:

- Protein 0.93g (2%),
- Potassium (K) 184 mg (4%) and
- Sodium, Na 2 mg (0%)

CILANTRO, CUCUMBER, AND LEMON INFUSION

Preparation time: 5 minutes

Cooking time: 5 minutes

Serving: 2

Ingredients:

1 quart (4 cups) filtered or spring water

1 piece, large lemon, use pulp only

1 piece, medium cucumber, ends removed, cubed into bite-sized pieces

1 sprig, knotted cilantro/coriander, rinsed well, drained

Directions:

1. Place all ingredients into a large pitcher. Mix while gently bruising fruits.

2. Set aside for at least an hour in the fridge. Strain out cilantro leaves. Pour drink. Consume liquid and fruits. Serve.

Nutrition:

- Protein 0.35g (1%),
- Potassium (K) 84 mg (2%) and
- Sodium, Na 11 mg (1%)

Preparation time: 5 minutes

Cooking time: 5 minutes

Serving: 2

Ingredients:

1 quart (4 cups) filtered or spring water

2 pieces, large lemons, use pulp only

1 sprig, knotted cilantro/coriander, rinsed well, drained

Directions:

1. Place all ingredients into a large pitcher. Mix while gently bruising lemons and cilantro leaves.
2. Set aside for at least an hour in the fridge. Strain out cilantro leaves. Pour drink. Consume liquid and fruits. Serve.

Nutrition:

- Protein 0.1g (0%),
- Potassium (K) 28 mg (1%) and
- Sodium, Na 5 mg (0%)

Preparation time: 5 minutes

Cooking time: 5 minutes

Serving: 2

Ingredients:

1 quart (4 cups) filtered or spring water

1 piece, large grapefruit peel, julienned, pulp squeezed

1 cup strawberries, quartered

Directions:

1. Place all ingredients into a large pitcher. Mix while gently bruising peels and fruits.
2. Set aside for at least an hour in the fridge. Strain out grapefruit peels. Pour drink. Consume liquid and strawberries. Serve.

Nutrition:

- Protein 0.59g (1%),
- Potassium (K) 130 mg (3%) and
- Sodium, Na 3 mg (0%)

STRAWBERRIES AND ELDERBERRY FLOWERS INFUSION

Preparation time: 5 minutes

Cooking time: 5 minutes

Serving: 2

Ingredients:

1 quart (4 cups) filtered or spring water

1 cup frozen strawberry, quartered

¼ cup elderberry flowers (salad-grade,) rinsed well, drained

Directions:

1. Place all ingredients into a large pitcher. Mix while gently bruising berries.
2. Set aside for at least an hour in the fridge. Strain out flowers. Pour drink. Consume liquid and berries. Serve.

Nutrition:

- Protein 0.3g (1%),
- Potassium (K) 107 mg (2%) and
- Sodium, Na 11 mg (1%)

SATSUMA INFUSION

Preparation time: 5 minutes

Cooking time: 5 minutes

Serving: 2

Ingredients:

1 quart (4 cups) filtered or spring water

½ pound Satsuma, peeled, remove pips (substitute Mandarin oranges)

Directions:

1. Place all ingredients into a large pitcher. Mix while gently bruising oranges.
2. Set aside for at least an hour in the fridge. Pour drink. Consume liquid and fruits. Serve.

Nutrition:

- Protein 0.46g (1%),
- Potassium (K) 94 mg (2%) and
- Sodium, Na 11 mg (1%)

ANTI-INFLAMMATORY SMOOTHIE

Preparation time: 3 minutes

Cooking time: 0 minutes

Serving: 2

Ingredients:

1 sprig mint

1/2 cup water

1/2 cup ice cubes

1 cup chopped cabbage

1 cup frozen peaches

1 cup white grapes

Directions:

1. Mix everything in a blender until smooth.
2. Serve in 4 glasses with a sprig of ice. Enjoy!

Nutrition:

- Calories: 48
- Protein: 1 g
- Sodium: 4 mg
- Potassium: 203 mg
- Phosphorus: 17 mg

Preparation time: 3 minutes

Cooking time: 5 minutes

Serving: 2

Ingredients:

1 cup low fat coconut milk

1 tbsp. stevia

2 cup filtered water

1 peeled and cored apple

1 pear

Directions:

1. Mix everything in a blender until smooth.
2. Serve in 4 glasses over ice. Enjoy!

Nutrition:

- Calories: 182
- Protein: 2 g
- Sodium: 14 mg
- Potassium: 300 mg
- Phosphorus: 70 mg

Preparation time:10 minutes

Cooking time:0 minutes

Serving:4

Ingredients:

3 ice cubes

1 tsp. honey

1/4 tsp. ground cinnamon

1/2 tsp. vanilla

1 cup unsweetened rice milk

1/2 cup chopped kale

1 cup blackberries

Directions:

1. Combine everything in a blender.

2. Blend until smooth.

3. Pour into 2 glasses. Serve and enjoy!

Nutrition:

- Calories: 118
- Protein: 2 g
- Sodium: 55 mg
- Potassium: 193 mg
- Phosphorus: 25 mg

BLUEBERRY SMOOTHIE

Preparation time: 5 minutes

Cooking time: 2 minutes

Serving: 3

Ingredients:

2 cups frozen blueberries (slightly thawed)

1 ¼ cup pineapple juice

2 tsp sugar or Splenda

¾ cup pasteurized egg whites

½ cup water

Directions:

1. Mix all the ingredients in blender and puree.

Nutrition:

- Protein - 7.4g
- Carbohydrates - 31.1g
- Fat - 0.75g
- Calories - 155.4

Preparation time:10 minutes

Cooking time:0 minutes

Serving:4

Ingredients:

1 cup coconut milk, canned

1 scoop Macadamia nuts butter

2 cups fresh spinach leaves, chopped

1/2 mango frozen or fresh

2 Tbsp stevia granulated sweetener to taste

1/2 cup water

1 cup ice cubes crushed

Directions:

1. Place Ingredients from the list above in your high-speed blender.
2. Blend for 35 - 50 seconds or until all ingredients are combined well.
3. Add less or more crushed ice.
4. Drink and enjoy!

Nutrition:

- Calories: 268
- Carbohydrates: 7g
- Proteins: 6g
- Fat: 26g
- Fiber: 1.5g

CHOCOLATE SMOOTHIE

Preparation time: 5 minutes

Cooking time: 5 minutes

Serving: 1

Ingredients:

1 tbsp cold water

1 tbsp powered Bakers Cocoa, unsweetened

2 cups ounces pasteurized liquid egg white

1 tbsp sugar

Chocolate bar shavings

4 tbsp whipped topping

Directions:

1. Combine sugar, cold water, and cocoa.
2. Stir until sugar dissolves.
3. Add 3 tablespoons of the whipped topping and egg whites.
4. Top with chocolate bar shavings and 1 tablespoon whipped topping.

Nutrition:

- Protein - 29 g
- Carbohydrates - 18 g
- Fat - 3 g
- Calories - 215

CREAMY DANDELION GREENS AND CELERY SMOOTHIE

Preparation time:10 minutes

Cooking time:0 minutes

Serving:4

Ingredients:

1 handful of raw dandelion greens

2 celery sticks

2 Tbsp chia seeds

1 small piece of ginger, minced

1/2 cup almond milk

1/2 cup of water

1/2 cup soy yogurt

Directions:

1. Rinse and clean dandelion leaves from any dirt; add in a high-speed blender.
2. Clean the ginger; keep only the inner part and cut into small slices; add in a blender.

3. Add all remaining ingredients and blend until smooth.

4. Serve and enjoy!

Nutrition:

- Calories: 58
- Carbohydrates: 5g
- Proteins: 3g
- Fat: 6g
- Fiber: 3g

COLLARD GREENS AND CUCUMBER SMOOTHIE

Preparation time: 10 minutes

Cooking time: 0 minutes

Serving: 4

Ingredients:

1 cup Collard greens

A few fresh peppermint leaves

1 big cucumber

1 lime, freshly juiced

1/2 cups fennel sliced

1 1/2 cup water

1 cup crushed ice

1/4 cup of natural sweetener Erythritol or Stevia (optional)

Directions:

1. Rinse and clean your Collard greens from any dirt.

2. Place all ingredients in a food processor or blender,

3. Blend until all ingredients in your smoothie are combined well.

4. Pour in a glass and drink. Enjoy!

Nutrition:

- Calories: 123
- Carbohydrates: 8g
- Proteins: 4g
- Fat: 11g
- Fiber: 6g

Preparation time: 10 minutes

Cooking time: 0 minutes

Serving: 2

Ingredients:

2 cups kale, torn

1 cup brewed green tea

1 cup pineapple chunks

1 cup cucumber, peeled and chopped

½ cup mango chunks, frozen

½ banana, peeled

1 teaspoon ground ginger

¼ teaspoon ground turmeric

3 mint leaves, chopped

1 tablespoon chia seeds

4 ice cubes

1 scoop protein powder

Directions:

1. In your blender, mix the kale with green tea, pineapple, cucumber, mango, banana, ginger, turmeric, mint, protein powder, and ice. Pulse well then add the chia seeds. Stir, divide into 2 glasses, and serve.

2. Enjoy!

Nutrition:

- Calories 161
- Fat 2 g
- Fiber 6 g
- Carbs 11 g
- Protein 5g

Preparation time:10 minutes

Cooking time:0 minutes

Serving:4

Ingredients:

3 ice cubes

1 tsp. honey

2 tsp. chia seeds

1 cup unsweetened rice milk

1/2 diced English cucumber

1 cup raspberries

Directions:

1. Combine everything in a blender.

2. Blend until smooth.

3. Pour into 2 glasses. Serve and enjoy!

Nutrition:

- Calories: 107
- Protein: 5 g
- Sodium: 42 mg
- Potassium: 135 mg
- Phosphorus: 37 mg

DARK TURNIP GREENS SMOOTHIE

Preparation time:10 minutes

Cooking time:0 minutes

Serving:4

Ingredients:

1 cup of raw turnip greens

1 1/2 cup of almond milk

1 Tbsp of almond butter

1/2 cup of water

1/2 tsp of cocoa powder, unsweetened

1/4 tsp of cinnamon

A pinch of salt

1/2 cup of crushed ice

Directions:

1. Rinse and clean turnip greens from any dirt.
2. Place the turnip greens in your blender along with all other ingredients.
3. Blend it for 45 - 60 seconds or until done; smooth and creamy.
4. Serve with or without crushed ice.

Nutrition:

- Calories: 131
- Carbohydrates: 6g
- Proteins: 4g
- Fat: 10g
- Fiber: 2.5g

FRESH CUCUMBER, KALE, AND RASPBERRY SMOOTHIE

Preparation time: 10 minutes

Cooking time: 0 minutes

Serving: 4

Ingredients:

1 1/2 cups of cucumber, peeled

1/2 cup raw kale leaves

1 1/2 cups fresh raspberries

1 cup of almond milk

1 cup of water

Ice cubes crushed (optional)

2 Tbsp natural sweetener (Stevia, Erythritol...etc.)

Directions:

1. Place all ingredients from the list in a food processor or high-speed blender; blend for 35 - 40 seconds.
2. Serve into chilled glasses.
3. Add more natural sweeter if you like. Enjoy!

Nutrition:

- Calories: 70
- Carbohydrates: 8g
- Proteins: 3g
- Fat: 6g
- Fiber: 5g

Fresh Lettuce and Cucumber-Lemon Smoothie

Preparation time:10 minutes

Cooking time:0 minutes

Serving:4

Ingredients:

2 cups fresh lettuce leaves, chopped (any kind)

1 cup of cucumber

1 lemon, washed and sliced.

1/2 fennel

2 Tbsp chia seeds

1 1/2 cup water or coconut water

1/4 cup stevia granulate sweetener (or to taste)

Directions:

1. Add all ingredients from the list above to the high-speed blender; blend until completely smooth.

2. Pour your smoothie into chilled glasses and enjoy!

Nutrition:

- Calories: 51
- Carbohydrates: 4g
- Proteins: 2g
- Fat: 4g
- Fiber: 3.5g

Preparation time: 10 minutes

Cooking time: 0 minutes

Serving: 4

Ingredients:

1 1/4 cup coconut milk (canned)

2 Tbsp chia seeds

1 cup of fresh kale leaves

1 cup of spinach leaves

1 scoop vanilla protein powder

1 cup ice cubes

Granulated stevia sweetener (to taste; optional)

1/2 cup water

Directions:

1. Rinse and clean kale and the spinach leaves from any dirt.
2. Add all ingredients to your blender.
3. Blend until you get a nice smoothie.
4. Serve into chilled glass.

Nutrition:

- Calories: 179
- Carbohydrates: 5g
- Proteins: 4g
- Fat: 18g
- Fiber: 2.5g

Preparation time: 10 minutes

Cooking time: 0 minutes

Serving: 4

Ingredients:

2 cups of instant coffee

1 cup almond milk (or coconut milk)

1/4 cup heavy cream

2 Tbsp cocoa powder (unsweetened)

1 - 2 Handful of fresh spinach leaves

10 drops liquid stevia

Directions:

1. Make a coffee; set aside.
2. Place all remaining ingredients in your fast-speed blender; blend for 45 - 60 seconds or until done.
3. Pour your instant coffee into a blender and continue to blend for a further 30 - 45 seconds.
4. Serve immediately.

Nutrition:

- Calories: 142
- Carbohydrates: 6g
- Proteins: 5g
- Fat: 14g
- Fiber: 3g

MANGO SMOOTHIE

Preparation time:10 minutes

Cooking time:0 minutes

Serving:4

Ingredients:

2 ice cubes

1 tsp. honey

2 tbsp. Basil nuts

1/2 cup chopped kale

1/2 mango chopped into cubes

1/2 chopped cucumber

1 cup water

Directions:

1. Combine everything in a blender.
2. Blend until smooth.

3. Pour into 2 glasses. Serve and enjoy!

Nutrition:
- Calories: 101
- Protein: 2 g
- Sodium: 11 mg
- Potassium: 200 mg
- Phosphorus: 63 mg

MINT LASSI

___

Preparation time:10 minutes

Cooking time:0 minutes

Serving:4

Ingredients:

1/2 cup water

1 cup unsweetened soy yogurt

1/2 cup mint leaves

1 tsp. cumin seeds

Directions:
1. Toast the cumin in a dry skillet until fragrant, about 1 to 2 minutes.
2. Add to a blender, along with the other ingredients, and process until smooth.
3. Divide into 2 glasses and serve. Enjoy!

Nutrition:
- Calories: 114
- Protein: 10 g
- Sodium: 43 mg
- Potassium: 179 mg
- Phosphorus: 158 mg

Preparation time: 3 minutes

Cooking time: 5 minutes

Serving: 2

Ingredients:

½ cup unsweetened almond milk

½ cup pineapple juice

½ cup low-cholesterol egg product

1 cup diced mango

Directions:

1. Put all the ingredients in a blender. Blend for 30 seconds.
2. Divide into 2 servings.
3. Serve.

Nutrition:

- Protein - 7 g
- Carbohydrates - 36 g
- Fat - 2 g
- Calories - 190

PINEAPPLE SMOOTHIE

Preparation time: 10 minutes

Cooking time: 0 minutes

Serving: 1

Ingredients:

1 cup of coconut water

1 canary melon, peeled and cut into cubes

1½ cups pineapple chunks

1 tablespoon fresh grated ginger

1 teaspoon chia seeds

1 teaspoon turmeric powder

A pinch of black pepper

Directions:

1. In your blender, mix the coconut water with the canary melon, pineapple, ginger, chia seeds, turmeric, and black pepper. Pulse well, pour into a glass, and serve for breakfast.
2. Enjoy!

Nutrition:

- Calories 151
- Fat 2 g
- Fiber 6 g
- Carbs 12 g
- Protein 4 g

PRETTY IN PINK SMOOTHIE

Preparation time: 10 minutes

Cooking time: 0 minutes

Serving: 4

Ingredients:

3 ice cubes

1/2 small, chopped, cooked beet

1 tsp. grated ginger

2 tsp. flax seed

1 cup unsweetened rice milk

1/2 chopped grapefruit

1 chopped pear

Directions:

1. Combine everything in a blender.
2. Blend until smooth.
3. Pour into 2 glasses. Serve and enjoy!

Nutrition:

Calories: 137

Protein: 2 g

Sodium: 50 mg

Potassium: 197 mg

Phosphorus: 37 mg

Preparation time: 10 minutes

Cooking time: 0 minutes

Serving: 2

Ingredients:

10 strawberries

¾ cup raspberry juice

¾ cup lime juice

½ cup raspberries

Directions:

1. In your blender, mix the strawberries with the raspberry juice, lime juice, and raspberries. Pulse well, divide into 2 glasses, and serve.
2. Enjoy!

Nutrition:

- Calories 125
- Fat 11 g
- Fiber 7 g
- Carbs 9 g
- Protein 3 g

Preparation time: 5 minutes

Cooking time: 5 minutes

Serving: 3

Ingredients:

1 medium peach, sliced

1 cup frozen raspberries

1 tablespoon honey

½ cup tofu

1 cup unfortified almond milk

Directions:

1. Mix all the ingredients in your blender.
2. Enjoy!

Nutrition:

- Protein - 6.3g
- Carbohydrates - 23g
- Fat - 3.2g
- Calories - 129

RASPBERRY AND PINEAPPLE SMOOTHIE

Preparation time: 5 minutes

Cooking time: 0 minutes

Serving: 4

Ingredients:

1 can, 8 oz, pineapple tidbits, rinsed well, drained

1 apple roughly chopped

½ cup frozen raspberries

½ cup crushed ice

Directions:

1. Except for cashew nuts and stevia, combine the remaining ingredients in a deep microwave-safe bowl. Stir.
2. Microwave on the highest setting for 5 to 15 seconds. Keep a watchful eye on this. Stop the cooking process before milk bubbles out of the bowl.
3. Carefully remove the bowl from the microwave. Cool slightly for easier handling.
4. Stir in stevia if using. Sprinkle cashew nuts.

Nutrition:

- Protein 3.1g (6%)
- Potassium (K) 749 mg (16 %)
- Sodium, Na 4 mg (0%)

Preparation time:10 minutes

Cooking time:0 minutes

Serving:4

Ingredients:

3 ice cubes

1/2 tsp. honey

1 tsp. vanilla

2 tbsp. cream cheese, at room temperature

1 cup hulled strawberries

1 cup unsweetened rice milk

Directions:

1. Combine everything in a blender.

2. Blend until smooth.

3. Pour into 2 glasses. Serve and enjoy!

Nutrition:

- Calories: 114
- Protein: 1 g
- Sodium: 102 mg
- Potassium: 132 mg
- Phosphorus: 33 mg

Preparation time:10 minutes

Cooking time:0 minutes

Serving:4

Ingredients:

1 cup ice

1 Peeled peach

2 cups watermelon chunks

Directions:

1. Combine everything in a blender.

2. Blend until smooth.

3. Pour into 2 glasses. Serve and enjoy!

Nutrition:
- Calories: 67
- Protein: 1 g
- Sodium: 3 mg
- Potassium: 278 mg
- Phosphorus: 28 mg

WINTER BERRY MILKSHAKE

Preparation time: 3 minutes

Cooking time: 5 minutes

Serving: 2

Ingredients:

3 ice cubes

1/2 cup blackberries

1/2 cup blueberries

1/ cup cranberries

1 cup unsweetened rice milk

Directions:
1. Combine everything in a blender.

2. Blend until smooth.

3. Pour into 4 glasses. Serve and enjoy!

Nutrition:
- Calories: 45
- Protein: 2 g
- Sodium: 29 mg
- Potassium: 118 mg
- Phosphorus: 33 mg

Preparation time: 4 minutes

Cooking time: 6 minutes

Serving: 1

Ingredients:

0,5 cups ounces of water

1 scoop whey protein powder

2 tbsp of Caramel Sugar-Free Syrup

6 ounces hot coffee

Directions:

1. Combine protein powder and water.

2. Stir in coffee and caramel syrup.

Nutrition:

*   Protein - 17 g

*   Carbohydrates - 1 g

*   Fat - 0 g

*   Calories - 72

CONCLUSION

I'd like to thank you and congratulate you for reading this book. I hope this book helped you understand what the renal failure diet is all about. You would have understood by now that it isn't just about following a diet for ensuring the health of your kidneys.

If you have got kidney sickness, decreasing your potassium, phosphorus, and sodium consumption can be a critical factor in coping with the disease.

I encourage you to return to this guidebook any time you are in doubt or whenever you would like to get back to useful tips on how to live a healthier life with damaged renal functions and chronic kidney disease. Make sure to always check your labels when shopping for groceries and take care that the meals you are preparing are made ready following the low-potassium and low-sodium diet for best results and remember that healthy habits make a healthy life.

Following a renal weight loss plan can seem daunting and a bit restrictive in instances. However, working along with your healthcare company and a renal dietitian will let you design a renal weight loss plan specific to your man or woman's desires.

Even if your disease has progressed to the point of receiving dialysis multiple times a week, using a renal diet can still work for you and help you feel better in your day to day life. You may not have even bought this book for yourself, but for someone else in your life that is experiencing chronic kidney disease, and that is noble and respected. You, whether for yourself or someone else, now have the tools that you need to plan, shop, and prepare meals that are healthy for your kidneys. If your kidneys are healthy and happy, the rest of your body is healthy and happy as well because it does not have to overwork itself or put unnecessary strain on other organs.

The next step is to apply everything you've learned here into your life. If you or loved ones are affected by CKD and other kidney problems, tell yourself/them that it is manageable especially during the early stages of the disease. You only need to follow your treatment regimen and live a healthy lifestyle. Include these kidney-friendly recipes in your meal plan and learn to embrace the renal diet lifestyle wholeheartedly.

Living with Chronic Kidney Disease (CKD) doesn't mean that your life is about to end. You can still live long without being unduly affected by the condition.

I wish you the best of luck!

NOTES

Made in the USA
Monee, IL
24 August 2023

41576025R10144